Boy at War

The Story of a Royal Navy
Volunteer Reserve Fighter
during the Second World War

By Lt (A) FJ George Boyd RNVR

Colourpoint

This story is dedicated to all those who served with 885 Squadron and in HMS *Ruler*, especially to those who, tragically, did not survive World War Two.

All rights reserved. No part of this publication may be reproduced, stored in a retrieval system or transmitted in any form or by any means, electronic, mechanical, photocopying, scanning, recording or otherwise, without the prior written permission of the copyright owners and publisher of this book.

6 5 4 3 2 1

© G Boyd and Colourpoint Books
Newtownards 2002

Designed by Colourpoint Books, Newtownards
Printed by Betaprint

ISBN 1 898392 06 4

About the Author

After the war, George Boyd was variously employed in Belfast as a stockbroker, a partner in AD MacIlwaine & Co for 30 years, and in life assurance and other financial services with Allied Dunbar Assurance for a further 17 years. He retired nine years ago. During this time he was a keen yatchsman, sailing mainly in the River Class at Strangford Lough Yacht Club. *Boyd's War* is his first book.

Cover Picture:
George Boyd and his Seafire over the Normandy beaches, June 1944 (Norman Whitla).

Colourpoint Books
Unit D5, Ards Business Centre
Jubilee Road
NEWTOWNARDS
County Down
Northern Ireland
BT23 4YH
Tel: 028 9182 0505
Fax: 028 9182 1900
E-mail: info@colourpoint.co.uk
Web-site: www.colourpoint.co.uk

Contents

Boyd's War		4
Prologue		6
1	Early War Days	10
2	Canada and New York	20
3	Operational Training	31
4	885 Royal Naval Air Squadron	42
5	Operation Overlord	50
6	Ulster	58
7	HMS *Ruler*	66
8	Australia	77
9	Pacific	86
10	Thoughts	101
11	Post-War	104
Appendices		106
Bibliography		118
Index		119

Note on Text Style

Roman type is used in respect of naval stations and italics for ship names, eg HMS Daedalus and HMS *King George V*.

Boyd's War

I did not shoot down dozens of enemy aircraft, so this is not a 'line-shoot'. It is intended to be a personal story of a Fleet Air Arm fighter pilot in World War Two. The reason I am putting my story down on paper is that I have been asked about various incidents by my children, grandchildren and others, and unless I put it down now I will have forgotten the incident, being a member of the CRAFT club ('Can't remember a flipping thing').

I should also add that neither is it a 'kiss and tell' story. That would take another book!

Oh Daddy what part in the war did you play,
What are the gongs you wear,
Not for firing a gun,
Or sinking the Hun,
But for sinking unlimited beer.

A Pilot my son was your Dad in the war,
A young man who had all the gen,
The wings of the Navy,
With rings that were wavy,
My motto was never say "when".

The worst part was always the waiting my son,
They never could realise the strain,
When poor throats were parched,
How slowly time marched,
Till they started the wine bills again.

A fine upright figure they thought me those days,
With guts and body of steel,
I was reckless and brave,
Even nonchalant save,
When signing the book for each meal.

But that's not the end of my daring exploits,
Your Father had nothing to hide,
He blitzed Normandy's highlands,
Some Japanese islands,
And the Cafe Moderne at Port Said.

   from *The Fleet Air Arm Song Book*

George Boyd
Killinchy
March 2002

Prologue

I was born on 4 March 1923 in Belfast, Northern Ireland. My father was a stockbroker in Belfast and the family lived in Princetown Road in Bangor, Co Down.

My father was a keen golfer, and had a large golf umbrella which I decided to try as a parachute when I was about six years old. (Our house was built on a slope and under the first floor at the back were garages and stores. The back door opened onto a balcony with steps down to ground level.) I placed a chair against the balcony railings and climbed up onto the top of the railings, holding the golf umbrella, and launched myself into the air. Half way to the ground the umbrella collapsed and I made a rather heavy and sore landing.

That incident put me off parachuting so much that many years later when I was invited to leave my aircraft by parachute I politely but firmly declined. Afterwards I just used the balcony for launching 'Frog' model aeroplanes and toy gliders.

As a small boy in Bangor I saw my first film one Saturday morning at the Adelphi Cinema in Main Street. The film was *Hell's Angels* with Jean Harlow. The entrance charge to this cinema on a Saturday morning was two jam jars. I was terribly impressed with this film; not with Jean Harlow, but with the aircraft and dog fights. For months after I spent a lot of time drawing tiny biplanes fighting all over the sky.

At an Alan Cobham's air circus, operating from a large field at nearby Groomsport, I spent the whole day, enthralled with the flying and the flying machines. These events helped me decide at an early age that I was going to be a fighter pilot rather than a train driver.

From my early days in Bangor I was involved in boating and sailing; my first efforts being on a plank in the pool when Pickie Pool was being built. I also rowed Laird's rowing skiffs in and out from their moorings when clients came to hire them, which I was forbidden to do by my mother.

I had at that time very light fair hair which made me very conspicuous in the bright sun and one day my mother saw me from a back window of the house, which overlooked the bay, rowing a skiff. She immediately rushed down to the jetty, grabbed me when I landed and frog-marched me home where I was whacked with a cane, which was kept on top of a large picture in the lounge.

When I was about fifteen my parents bought me an International 14 footer Uffa Fox sailing dinghy costing £18, which I learnt to sail at Bangor and later at Whiterock.

Every summer my family would close up the Bangor house and move to Whiterock on the shores of Strangford Lough. They went by car and my brother and I went by bicycle. The Newtownards straight, part of the Ulster TT car racing circuit, was a very tough cycle ride with the wind against you.

My early sailing at Whiterock was quite basic. I would row a dinghy up the bay into the wind and at the top of the bay I would stick an oar through a hole in the thwart, hoist an old sheet on it and sail downwind to the other end of the bay.

I became a boarder at Mourne Grange prep school at Kilkeel. Here 'non singers' had to do carpentry, in lieu of choir practice, which suited me perfectly. I built a flat bottomed punt, a canoe and a pair of sea walking shoes, which were a pair of elongated boxes about six feet long and one foot wide with a pair of old gym shoes nailed on top. I have to admit that the sea walking shoes were a failure.

During my early days in Bangor I remember watching the big 'J' class yachts racing. Two that I remember were *Britannia*, King George V's yacht, and *Shamrock V*, owned by Sir Thomas Lipton, who made his challenge for the Americas' Cup race from the Royal Ulster Yacht Club at Bangor of which he was a member. He had been refused membership of any English 'Royal' Yacht Club because he was by trade, a grocer!

Another exciting event in Bangor was the yearly visit of some of

J Class yachts racing off Bangor in the 1930s.

Strangford Lough Yacht Club at Whiterock.

our battleships and battlecruisers which were open to the public. I was all over *Nelson* and *Rodney* and many other ships.

Another big event each year was the Ulster TT motor race around the Ards circuit. We watched Earl Howe (Bugatti), Nuvolari, Freddie Dixon (Riley), Kay Don (Lea Francis), Freddie Hall (Bentley), Carrickiola and Reg Parnell, not to mention Prince Bira of Siam. At one of the races I was fortunate enough to get Jimmy O'Dea's autograph – he was a famous Irish comedian.

Whiterock was the home of the Snipe Sailing Club and I used to crew in a Snipe class sailing boat. The clubhouse was a wooden structure which burnt down one night and was eventually replaced by the Strangford Lough Yacht Club.

The River class boats sailed here and Lord Londonderry and his family sailed two of them, *Ulagh* and *Gwebarra*. When Count von Ribbentrop stayed with the Londonderrys at Mount Stewart, on the other side of the Lough, he sailed with them in their Rivers.

I sailed my International 14-footer regularly at Whiterock and won my first race at Whiterock Regatta, for which the prize was £1. With this huge bounty I was able to buy a large black oilskin coat.

When Neville Chamberlain made his broadcast, declaring war on Germany, I heard it in the Strangford Lough Yacht Club, having just come in from sailing. I was on holiday from my school in Scotland.

Chapter 1
Early War Days

I was attending Loretto School, Musselburgh, in Scotland when war broke out. Musselburgh was about ten miles east of Edinburgh on the Firth of Forth with the River Esk flowing through the town. Near the mouth of the river there was a footbridge to our playing fields at Newfield.

At Loretto, as at Mourne Grange, 'non singers' were required to do carpentry in lieu of choir practice, so I built another canoe which I stored in slings under the Newfield footbridge. Then, when the tide was suitable, another like-minded boy and I would get up at dawn and go canoeing for a few hours in the Firth of Forth before the school woke up.

During the first German air raid on the Forth Bridge and Rosyth we were all taking shelter in slit trenches which we had recently dug at the seaward end of the Newfield playing fields. Several of our Spitfire fighters were firing at a German bomber which turned low over us with smoke pouring out of one engine and crashed a mile or so out to sea. We later heard that one of our pilots who claimed the kill was an old boy of Loretto, operating from nearby RAF airfield at Drem. Some excitement for us all!

While at Loretto I nearly got expelled for running a betting syndicate. Because we were successful our winnings arrived by registered post addressed to one member of our syndicate, each in turn. When our winnings reached a certain level the well-known bookmaker, McLean of Glasgow, with whom we dealt and who knew our headmaster personally, tipped him off that there was a betting ring operating in the school. He would not give names as that would be disclosing a confidence!; but it was easy for the head' to check the names of the half dozen or so boys who regularly received registered letters.

As I was the leader I was going to be expelled and the head' wanted to tell my father who was due over in Edinburgh for the Scottish–Irish rugby match at Murrayfield the next day. My father duly arrived down to see the head' and when told the story he said: "What are you worrying about, weren't they winning." Much to my relief, instead of being expelled I was promoted to a school prefect.

During the school holidays we were expected to help the 'Dig for Victory' campaign by working on farms. I worked at Whiterock during the day for our local farmer, weeding parsley from six in the morning to six in the evening. This entailed crawling up the drills with bags on your knees, weeding the drills by hand, a very arduous task, and all for 18s per week (90p).

Also during the school holidays we were expected to join our Local Defence Force. I joined the Killinchy LDF which became the Royal Ulster Constabulary 'B' Specials and later the Home Guard – now known as 'Dad's Army' thanks to the popular BBC comedy series.

At Loretto I was also a sergeant in the OTC (Officer Training Corps.), and when we formed the ATC (Air Training Corps), I became a Flight Sergeant in it.

When I first attended the Killinchy LDF squad, they were drilling with broom sticks, pitch forks, etc. By the following holidays they had some arms but no knowledge of how to use them. As a trained OTC Sergeant, capable of stripping down and reassembling, blindfolded, a Lewis gun and a Bren gun, I offered to instruct. This was not acceptable as they did not think it right for a 17 year old to be instructing older members of the squad. Having said that, I would add that the last time I joined them they had become a most efficient and well trained Home Guard squad. By that time, they were trained by the Welsh Regiment stationed in adjacent Killyleagh who trained them. As in *Dad's Army*, the Home Guard leader was the local bank manager, Joe Kelly.

I have two incidents to record of my Home Guard duty. One night on one of our road-block duties, a car failed to stop at the red light shown by our patrol at Killinchy crossroads and roared off in the direction of Comber. So, as directed, I knelt in the middle of the road and fired five rounds of .303 after him, which did not stop him. I never heard anything more of this incident so I presume I must have missed him with all shots.

On another occasion another member and I were in a post on top of a prominent hill known as the 'Knowe Head'. It was a pitch-dark night and our instructions were to watch for any lights or unusual activity in or around Strangford Lough. We were to challenge anyone approaching us other than by the lane in front. At about two o'clock in the morning we heard footsteps and heavy breathing coming from the field behind our post. We issued our three challenges, and receiving no response, we each fired three rounds in the direction of the noise. Then, out of the fog and darkness, appeared two cows, both I am glad to say uninjured.

At this time I was the proud owner of a 250cc James 2-stroke grass-track motorbike and I used this to take me from Whiterock up to the Killinchy Orange hall for Home Guard parades. I was always late because of the difficulty in getting the machine started, which had to be done by pushing and jumping on. I would be decked out in my hot serge uniform, Lee Enfield .303 rifle, loaded bandoleer of ammunition, tin hat and gas mask slung around me, and being pushed by all the family. When the machine fired, the squad could hear it up in Killinchy and knew that I was on my way.

My contemporaries at school and I were all very impatient to get into the war but we had to wait until we were 18. To try to get round this we all applied in writing to join the Royal Navy, the Royal Air Force and the Indian Army (because you could start as a Lieutenant at Bangalore if you had School's Certificate, which we all had or would have shortly), hoping that one of them would call us up before we were 18.

Alas, none of these did call us up, so I decided to go to the Combined Recruiting Centre in Edinburgh to join the Royal Navy (Air Branch) on my birthday, 4 March 1941.

I was certain this was the Service for me. A few days before that I had spoken by phone to Frank Hollywood, an old friend in Bangor, who asked me to wait until 20 March, his birthday, when he would come over to Edinburgh and we could join up together. Reluctantly I agreed to this delay and that is what happened. Our plan worked in that we did our training together for a year. Having signed on at 18, we still had to wait to be called for interview and this did not happen for some months, during which time we practiced our interview technique.

One day I was invited out to lunch at the Union Club, Belfast, by Austin Boyd, the owner of Old Bushmills Distillery, to meet a Fleet Air Arm pilot who was ashore from a 'camship'. This was a ship which carried one Hurricane fighter on a catapult which was launched in mid Atlantic to try to shoot down German Condor reconnaissance aircraft, after which they had to 'ditch' in the sea alongside the ship and hope to be picked up. He told me that the survival rate in the Fleet Air Arm at that time was 50/50. Rather than put me off, this only made me more impatient to get into it.

Shortly after this, Bangor was bombed. One bomb landed on the entrance pillar of a house two doors down Princetown Road from our house. All our windows were blown in, or out, but fortunately I had got all the family to lie under the large dining-room table just before the bomb arrived, so no one was injured. My family evacuated to the cottage at Whiterock, leaving me to clear up the mess and board up the windows.

The following day Frank Hollywood and I got our orders to attend for interview at Royal Naval Barracks, Portsmouth. We travelled from Larne to Stranraer and then by train to London and Portsmouth. It took us a long time to reach Portsmouth due to air raids all along the line.

When we eventually reported to RN Barracks, Portsmouth, there was an air raid in progress and we were directed to an air raid shelter, running the length of the huge parade ground, where we stayed for most of the night. A similar air raid shelter on the other side of the parade ground received a direct hit and nearly all in it were killed. That was our welcome to the Royal Navy!

Next morning we were interviewed by a half dozen or so senior RN officers and one pilot RNVR (A) officer. The RNVR (A) officer had sailed at the Royal North of Ireland Yacht Club at Cultra, and when he asked me if I knew it I was able to tell him that I sailed as crew in a Dragon class yacht there. That was not the only reason I got in. I managed to answer most of the questions and – thanks to my practice interview training at school – I got through, as did Frank Hollywood. We then had to go through all sorts of medicals and tests after which we both passed as Pilot or Observer. We both chose to train as pilots. We were sent home again to await being called up for training.

As there was no conscription in Northern Ireland, we were volunteers and in the Royal Naval Volunteer Reserve for 'hostilities only'. As we had joined for flying duties as pilots we were posted to HMS Daedalus at Lee-on-Solent, the assembly point for aircrew trainees.

On arrival we were kitted out as Naval Airmen 2nd class. The 'rig' or dress was an ordinary seaman's uniform with a white band round the cap. We were here for a few weeks painting the stones around the parade ground white and other silly and tedious duties.

At this time actors like Ralph Richardson, Laurence Olivier and also Peter Cadbury of the well-known chocolate company were all based at Lee-on-Solent. They had private pilot's licenses before the war and owned their own aircraft so they flew them into Lee and joined up there. We were then moved to HMS St Vincent at Gosport. We were part of a course of 60, half of whom were from New Zealand, with Frank Hollywood, Harry Clendinning, and myself from Northern Ireland, Bill Wallace and Pat Sherry from the Irish Free State and the rest English.

St Vincent was 'ruled' by Chief Petty Officer Wilmot, a naval gunnery petty officer from Whale Island. We were formed into small squads with one of us in charge in turn, and had to double march all over the place. When going from one place to another it had to be done at the double. Everywhere were hung slogans of Nelson's signals such as "Engage the enemy more closely," and "England expects" etc.

At the front of the main building at St Vincent there was a huge mast from an old sailing ship rigged with yards, ratlines and a crow's nest etc. As part of the course we were required to climb to the top yard. As I suffer from vertigo (fear of heights) I thought I would be caught out on this. However, a good friend helped me out. We both climbed to the first level where I remained and he went on, came down again, I slipped round to the other side of the mast and he went up and down again which satisfied the instructor as the

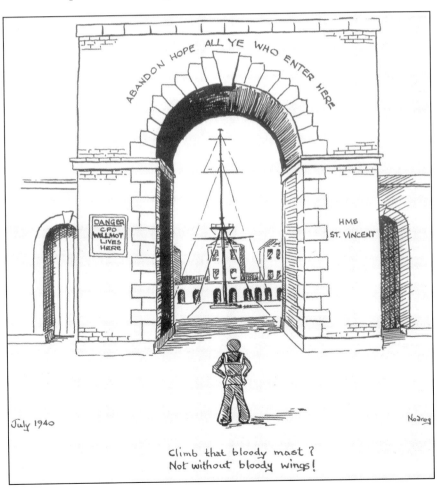

correct number had gone up and down.

I have been asked many times how someone suffering from vertigo could be a pilot. The simple answer is that when flying you are not attached to the ground, which makes all the difference. It is a fact that a large proportion of pilots suffer from vertigo.

The course lasted about three months consisting of classroom studies and basic training in seamanship, navigation, airmanship, theory of flight, meteorology and the internal combustion engine. Another subject was, much to our amusement, called OLQ (officer-like qualities). Boat-pulling practice was performed in Portsmouth Harbour in freezing weather. It seemed a bit odd to be crewing a whaler around Portsmouth Harbour when we had joined to learn how to fly aeroplanes.

When we did get overnight leave, after a few pints in Gosport, Pompey (naval and football slang for Portsmouth) or Southsea, we could always get a bed and breakfast at a 'Maggie Weston' hostel for sailors for 1s (5p) per night. Our pay at that time was 2s 6d (12.5p) per day. (Maggie Weston's was a hostel for poor sailors set up many years ago by a benefactress of that name, and were to be found in most ports around the UK.)

When crossing from Pompey to Gosport, I remember seeing an old 'J' class hulk lying afloat at a boat yard, and I heard after the war that some keen yachtsman had rebuilt her to her former glory.

We 'passed out' of St Vincent as acting leading naval airmen, with the 'killick' (anchor) badge displayed on the arm of our jumpers.

Our course was now transferred to 24 EFTS (Elementary Flying Training School) run by the RAF at Short Brothers' grass airfield at Sealand, just outside Chester.

An important aspect of finally getting to the flying stage was that promotion from naval airmen 2nd class to acting leading naval airmen, with flying pay, meant a pay rise. We now received the princely sum of 6s 9d per day (34p).

At Sealand we were to learn to fly de Havilland Tiger Moth

biplanes equipped with 100 hp Gypsy Major engines. They had two cockpits, one behind the other and open to the weather! At night the Tiger Moths were dispersed around the perimeter of the airfield and tied down to concrete blocks with rings in them. First thing in the morning we then had to untie the lashings, hoist the tail of the aircraft onto our shoulders and march off with the aircraft to our flight hut.

We were kitted out with very cumbersome flying clothing – a thick canvas overall, a pair of silk gloves, a pair of leather gauntlets (the reason for these was the better to deal with fire in the cockpit), a pair of fleece-lined flying boots, and a leather helmet and goggles. All these were necessary as we were flying in aircraft with open cockpits and it was very cold. The helmet had 'Gosport Tubes' fitted, which were plugged into similar tubes in the aircraft through which you communicated with your instructor. Altogether it was a rather hazardous means of communication as, with the engine noise and the slipstream noise, it was most difficult to hear at times.

The author

On 24 April 1942 I had my first flight in a Tiger Moth, the biplane on which we were to train. The training was pretty intense – any pilot who did not go solo in about ten hours dual instruction was 'washed out' and sent off to other naval duties.

I was greatly relieved to find that my vertigo had no effect once I was in the air.

One of the most frightening parts of the training was that, as soon as you took off, you were taught to look out for a suitable field on which to make a forced landing should your engine fail. Another shaker was to climb to several thousand feet, switch off the engine and then dive to re-start it from the airstream.

On the morning of 14 May, with just ten hours dual flying, my instructor told me that I was landing too high and not to throttle back until I could see the individual blades of grass. He also told me I was too heavy on the rudder and suggested that I take off my shoes and socks and throw them over the side. This I did and he made me do another landing bare footed, which was faultless. He then climbed out of his cockpit and sent me off on my first solo flight. Marvellous!

I found that sailing and flying were very similar, back-filling your sail was very like stalling an aircraft. I also found that once in the air you had a strong superiority complex, looking down on the tiny figures below.

As well as blind flying exercises in the air, wearing a hood over the cockpit, we spent hours in the 'link trainer.' The link trainer was a box-like piece of equipment with a completely enclosed cockpit which simulated actual flying. It was fitted with the usual controls and a full instrument panel, and when you were aboard it bounced you around like a bucking bronco in total darkness. It was very sensitive to careless handling and any ham-handed movement of the stick would stall it and even spin it. It was much more difficult to fly than a real aircraft.

Air navigation was an essential part of the syllabus, and this allowed us to land at other airfields on cross-country flights.

Every month we were rated as to 'Proficiency as Pilot,' the three ratings being 'above average', 'average' and 'below average.' I had learnt in my early flying career that to survive one should remain 'average' because the 'above average' and 'below average' pilots usually wrote themselves off.

The rest of the flying syllabus followed up to 17 June by which time I had flown 71 hours and passed out rated 'average.'

The social life at Sealand was superb. Most nights there was a bus laid on into Chester, a town with a large number of good pubs and a fine hotel. There was also a large hospital complex and an abundance of beautiful nurses. We spent many hours paddling up the River Dee to the Iron Bridge and back in canoes and rowing skiffs with these nurses.

The de Havilland Tiger Moth.

Rowing canoes at the Iron Bridge, Chester. The author in the stern and Frank Hollywood in the bow.

Chapter 2
Canada and New York

After leave and some time waiting around the course embarked in the troop ship *Letitia*. On this passage she was grossly overcrowded and this was my first experience of sleeping in a hammock, very uncomfortable for people of my height (six foot) as one's heels dug into the clews (ropes holding the canvas). We zig-zagged across the Atlantic for three weeks, sometimes up among the icebergs, and sometimes down in the hot weather. Our convoy eventually arrived in Halifax, Nova Scotia.

It is quite a coincidence that the same ship, the liner *Letitia*, went aground on the South Briggs rocks near Orlock in 1935, just a few miles from where I lived in Bangor. She was on passage from Montreal, Canada, to Belfast. They managed to refloat her after three or four days.

Postcard showing the Letitia *grounded in 1935.*

Members of No 60 Naval Pilots Course.

Norman Rodgers Airfield near Kingston, Ontario, Canada.

From the left: Harry Clendinning, Jeff Parker and the author.

We disembarked at Moncton in New Brunswick, a very cold place. We heard later that *Letitia* was torpedoed and sunk on her next trip. After a few days at Moncton we made a two-day train journey to Kingston, Ontario. Kingston is situated at the 'top' end of Lake Ontario. The Thousand Islands and the International Bridge are a few miles up the St Lawrence from Kingston.

Our base was about six miles down the lake from Kingston at the Norman Rodgers airfield, named after one of Canada's early aviators. We were to join No 31 SFTS (Service Flying Training School), where we were to learn to fly American Harvard IIs advanced trainers equipped with very noisy Wasp S3HI engines. After the Tiger Moths these were real aircraft – big, fast, and with landing flaps and a retractable undercarriage.

I had my first Harvard flight on 20 July 1942 and finished the course on 4 November 1942, by which time I had 208 hours in my log book.

The CO of the unit was Group Captain Mackworth, famous among flyers as the winner of the 1936 Schneider Trophy. The Supermarine aircraft, which he flew in that race, was the forerunner to the Spitfire.

For air firing practice a canvas 'drogue' was towed around by a Lysander aircraft and we had to fire at the 'drogue'. The drogue-towing pilot of the station was the then unknown Jimmy Edwards, later to become a well-known comedian.

The item that made an initial impression on me in Canada was the whiter than white bread we got there – a contrast to the mixed-grain off-white bread we had become accustomed to at home.

31 SFTS Kingston, Ontario, Canada. 17/07/42 – 06/11/42

I must say here that the Canadian hospitality was superb. Families all around and in Kingston opened their homes to us.

On arrival at Kingston we three Ulstermen – Frank Hollywood, Harry Clendinning and myself – bought a six-cylinder 1923 Nash Coupe for $60 (Canadian). It broke down on the way back to camp and we had to abandon it on the roadside. We did not get back to it for a week and when we did the windscreen was covered with parking tickets amounting to hundreds of dollars.

We ignored these and had opened the bonnet to try to get the thing going when up drove a motorcycle speed cop, complete with the hexagonal cap, belt and holsters, pistol and handcuffs, etc. He said, "Are you the owners of this car, which has been parked here for the past week?" I started to explain what had happened, whereupon he said "How far from Belfast do you live?" When I told him, he held out his hand and said "My name is Crawford and I'm from Ballymena. Let's see what's wrong." He took off his guns and jacket and sorted out the twin

George Crawford, a native of Ballymena and Kingston's speed cop.

blocked carburettors in a few minutes. I had not realised my Ulster accent was so obvious!

He then escorted us to the City Hall to have our parking tickets dealt with by their equivalent of an RM, whose name was Maginnis, a millionaire contractor of Irish descent who had actually built our runways. He immediately cancelled our parking tickets and invited us home to his mansion between Kingston and our base for a fantastic dinner. There we met his two daughters who had much better cars than our Coupe. We were invited to drop in anytime we were off and this we often did. We had many barbecues and swimming sessions at his private dock on Lake Ontario.

In order to pay for the gasoline for our car we ran a taxi service into Kingston on our nights and days off.

I also had a very enjoyable weekend trip with our policeman friend, Crawford, to his bungalow on Prince Edward Bay, between Kingston and Toronto.

On another weekend I hitch-hiked to Toronto and was picked up by a gentleman who lived in a small town off the main highway. As it was getting dark when we came to his turn off, he very kindly invited me home with him for the night. I met his wife, (there were no children), and we had a great night's crack. He left me down to the highway the next morning and told me on the way down that if I would like to come back after the war he would give me a good job in his printing business, with a view to taking over as he had no family. I did not take him up on this offer, one good reason being that the cold there in the winter is so intense that someone like me with big ears would suffer a lot.

On one of our car trips over the International Bridge to Watertown in New York state, the Canadian customs men searched us and confiscated $91 (Canadian) which I had in my cap. We thought that a bit mean, applying their exchange control regulations to a few underpaid trainee pilots. It was the only bad incident during our otherwise enjoyable stay in Canada. When we were leaving Canada it was in the depth of winter and we could not sell the car to the incoming course. So we had to drive it to the scrap heap and got $60 (Canadian) for it, the original cost.

Towards the end of the course we went to Gananoque, a tented airfield at the end of the International Bridge over the St Lawrence River, for night flying training. It is very difficult to sleep in a tent when noisy Harvard aircraft are taking off and landing over you all night. Night flying in Canada was so much easier because there was no 'black out' there, such as we were used to in the UK, so that it was always possible to see some lights that would show you that you were flying the right way up. Navigation in Canada was totally different from what we were used to in the UK. Here you navigated by the high-tension cables cut through the hundreds and hundreds of square miles of forest. My Harvard flying hours were now Dual 19.45 and Pilot 50.30

At Kingston, Harry Clendinning and I had two sisters as our regular girlfriends; Harry's was called Nadine. Some years later, after the war, Harry visited Caproni's ballroom in Bangor one Saturday night and was amazed to see Nadine dancing there. He discovered that Nadine had married a chap from Bangor who was on the course after us and now she lived with him in Bangor.

A favourite song at Kingston was 'Mr Pupil and Mr Instructor':

Oh, Mr. Instructor – Oh, Mr. Instructor,
Can you tell me how my flying's been assessed?
Though I spin out of control,
When I try a half flick roll,
A guy can do no better than his best.

Oh, Mr. Pupil – Oh, Mr. Pupil,
Say, your best is not quite good enough for me.
You'll enjoy much better health,
In a thing that rolls itself.
A Marlet, Mr. Instructor?

Squadron formation over the St Lawrence.

Good brakes and bad brakes!

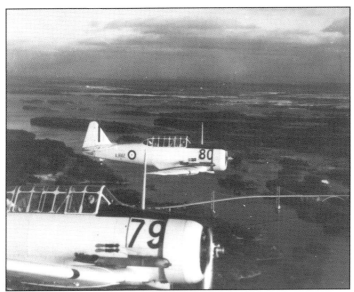
Harvards over the International Bridge, Ontario, Canada.

Number 80 returning to Gananoque Field with Gananoque town in the background.

In a corvette, Mr. P.
Oh Mr. Instructor, Yes Mr. Pupil?
These precautionary landings are a bore.
Now I'm holding off at last,
Only three feet from the grass,
Can you tell me what that horn is sounding for?

Oh Mr. Pupil, Oh Mr. Pupil,
There's a handle on the left side don't you see.
If that handle's not pressed down,
You'll land too close to the ground.
A three-pointer, Mr. Instructor?
On your belly, Mr. P.

from *The Fleet Air Arm Song Book*

(There is a lot more, but I won't bore you with that.)

At the end of the course, having got my 'Wings' and with about a week's leave, I hitch-hiked down to New York. My last hitch let me off at five in the morning at the bow of the French liner *Normandy* which was lying on her side in the dock. There had been a fire on board and the fire fighters had pumped so much water into her that she capsized.

Here I was picked up by a New York policeman who would not believe that I was a naval aviator until I took off my rating's overcoat and showed him my 'Wings' on the sleeve of my jumper. He took me into an all night cafe nearby and stood me many cups of coffee until it was light and time for me to go on up town.

The New York hospitality was also superb. I was given tickets for the 'stage door canteen' and danced with Dorothy Lamour there, albeit for a few minutes, before a large 'gob' (American sailor) interrupted.

I then contacted an Ulsterman, Chris Smiles, brother of Sir Walter

Smiles, who took me to his house at Hartford, Connecticut, where I was very well entertained. Chris's wife, Imelda, produced a beautiful red-headed niece of her's for my partner. Apart from all the parties he arranged here, I had to lecture his friends in their equivalent of our Home Guard, but there were no reservations such as I had experienced at Killinchy.

I also contacted a New York stockbroker with whom my father dealt, a Mr Wolfson of Heyden Stone, and he took me out to lunch in a famous restaurant with a great hole in the outer wall, which had been caused by a British shell when our ships shelled New York during the War of 1812. It is a bit like the Battle of the Boyne here in Ireland; it has never been forgotten.

During my first day in New York, I had bought a bus ticket to Quebec in case I ran out of money. The reason I wanted to go to Quebec was that I had a contact from Belfast to meet there. I used this ticket and met up with Mr Francis, a retired director of the Headline Shipping Co (based in Belfast), who very generously entertained me for a few days before sending me back to Kingston by train. While in Quebec I also visited Austin Boyd's wife and two young sons who had been evacuated to Canada at the start of the war.

Back at Kingston we then had a long train journey to join the *Queen Elizabeth* for the return passage to the UK, embarking from New York. The *QE* drove at full speed through one of the worst North Atlantic storms ever recorded and made the Clyde in only four days. With 15,000 US troops aboard, conditions were appalling and the vast majority were violently seasick. Fortunately I did not succumb to this and was better fed than ever before, that is when I could catch the plates flying up and down the mess tables.

I was in charge of No 18 lifeboat on the port side aft. I had several members of the ship's crew to help me launch. I obviously had not a clue, but after a few 'boat drills' I was beginning to get the hang of the lifeboat launching procedures.

On arrival at Greenock we got leave just in time for Christmas.

Although we got our 'Wings' (the coveted badge of a pilot) in Canada, we were not commissioned in the Fleet Air Arm until we were back in the UK. Those of us like myself who had not attained the age of 20 had to accept the rank of midshipman for the time being, which was a bit galling, since all those over 20 were sub-lieutenants with higher pay although they had done the exact same course.

Midshipman Boyd

Chapter 3
Operational Training

04/01/43 – 23/01/43

In our new uniforms we now had to report to No 9 AFU at Errol, Perthshire, to convert back to British aircraft types. These were Masters Mk1 with Kestrel engines and Mk11 with Mercury engines, and were good to fly.

We had very bad weather at Errol with cloud, snow, fog and rain, quite a change from the blue skies of Ontario. One day one of our course with his instructor flew into a hill in fog. The instructor was killed and our colleague seriously injured.

Whilst here, we used to go into Perth most evenings and, invariably, missing the last train back, we walked the railway sleepers back to camp. I can assure you that the distance between railway sleepers is not designed for walking with a normal stride.

At this time we sadly heard of the death of Frank Hollywood who had crashed in a Hurricane in Wales. Frank and I had been together from joining up until this last posting, when I went to Errol and Frank to Wales.

Sub-Lts HG Clendinning and DFA Hollywood RNVR

22/02/43 – 28/05/43

Having been selected for 'fighter' training, my next appointment was to the Fighter School at HMS Heron, RNAS Yeovilton, 759 Squadron.

The CO here had his own Gloster Gladiator, a beautiful little biplane fighter in which he used to take off every morning to do a

Gloster Gladiator

Sea Hurricanes at RNAS Yeovilton.

Fairey Fulmar

weather test.

On 25 February 1943 I had my first solo in a Hurricane, which nearly ended in disaster.

After a normal take-off I opened the throttle wide to see how she would go. It was like getting a thump in the back and I gained about 2000 feet before I had proper control again. When I had got over the heady excitement of flying such a powerful machine I looked around and could see no landmarks that I recognised.

I flew around for a while and realised I was lost and getting very short of fuel. I had no radio contact as my radio had given up. I noticed a small grass airfield on the top of a hill and landed. I was refuelled and phoned my instructor who told me to wait until he flew over and then to take off and follow him. I was very glad to do this and get back to base and relax. There were some very good pubs near Yeovilton, 'The Lamb and Lark' within walking distance across some fields and 'The Bull' in nearby Ilchester.

We also had 'escape and evasion' training which was great fun. We would be taken out blindfolded in the back of a lorry for a distance of ten miles from the camp and dumped, with no money or identification, and had to find our way back to camp without speaking any English. We were allowed to steal bicycles and cars if we found any not immobilised. One of our blokes stole an aircraft from an RAF airfield and flew it back to Yeovilton. Needless to say, the RAF were not amused.

Training on Hurricanes went on up to mid April when I transferred to the advanced flight for deck landing training, night flying and live air-firing. This flight was equipped with Mk11 Fairey Fulmars and Sea Hurricanes. The Fulmar was a gentleman's aircraft where you could wear your cap with earphones over, it rather than the usual helmet, and it was equipped with a funnel in a tube through which you could have a pee.

At this time we did a lot of ADDLs (airfield dummy deck landings) in preparation for landing on an aircraft carrier. In this a 'batsman' stood at the side of the end of the runway with two 'bats'

ADDLs – Lower!

ADDLs – Throttle up!

ADDLs – Round again!

The 'Fulmar Boys'

The Fleet Air Arm (FAA) at work!

with which he indicated you were making too high an approach, by lowering the bats, or that you were coming in too low, by raising the bats. The object was to land and 'cut' (throttle back) alongside 'Bats'. For hours we did 'circuits and bumps' and after each touch down we would open the throttle wide and take off again for the next circuit.

On 17 May the course went up to Scotland by train to try the real thing on an aircraft carrier. On 19 and 29 May I did my first five deck landings on HMS *Argus* in the Clyde in a Fairey Fulmar (*Argus* was a 'leftover' from World War One and the flight deck seemed to us a long way above the sea). Quite an experience! I managed OK as did the rest of the course, without any prangs.

After this Scottish adventure we returned to Yeovilton and back onto Hurricanes to do an 'air firing' course at the Naval Air Firing unit at Warmwell. Here Martinets (adapted Masters) towed target 'drogues' over the range off Chesil Beach and we carried out 'quarter attacks' on the drogues. At first it was quite frightening when you pressed the firing button on the Hurricane's control column to feel the aircraft judder and slow in speed under the heavy recoil of the eight guns in the aircraft's wings.

The Yeovilton Fighter Course finished in early June when we went on two weeks leave. By this time I had a total of 288 hours flying in my log book and was hoping that my next appointment would be to an operational squadron.

Instead of being posted to an operational squadron – the reason I had volunteered – I was posted to a 'stooge' squadron. I understand this was because the expansion of the Fleet Air Arm had now reached a point where the supply of newly trained pilots was in excess of the supply of aircraft.

19/06/43 – 07/10/43

In June 1943 I joined HMS Kestrel, RNAS Worthy Down, near Winchester. Worthy Down was a small grass airfield with a hillock in the middle. My task was to train TAGs (telegraphist/air gunners) flying Proctors in 756 Squadron and Lysanders in 755 Squadron.

This was a very comfortable job but not what I had joined for. It was a nine to five job with every other weekend off, when we would go up to London. This turned out to be very expensive after a while.

On one of my weekends in London I was walking along Leicester Square when I met Douglas MacIlwaine, also from Bangor and my partner after the war in stockbroking. With him was a New Zealand naval officer who had been with him on a course on gunnery at Whale Island. The three of us adjourned to a local pub for a few pints and then went to see *Gone With The Wind*.

On another occasion I was walking through Trafalgar Square when a sailor tapped me on the shoulder and on turning round I found my brother Tom whom I had not seen for several years. He was a submariner and had just returned from Norwegian waters. We had quite a celebration before going our separate ways again.

On a third occasion, this time in Pompey (Portsmouth), I ran into Arthur Neill, an old friend from Bangor. He had just come back from Norfolk, Virginia, USA, where his ship, the battleship HMS *Warspite*, was being repaired. Not having seen each other for some years we naturally celebrated in a nearby pub.

On TAG training work a very young sailor would have to keep in W/T (wireless telegraphy) touch with base for as long as he could, while I flew the aircraft away from base for a distance of a hundred miles. Very often these poor boys were airsick and I would tell them to be sick into their hats and not dirty the interior of my aircraft. One advantage of this job from my point of view was that I saw a lot of southern England from the air and had very good practice in navigation and map reading.

One evening I visited a pub near to Worthy Down and was amazed to see Judy C, a girl from Bangor whom I had rather fancied. She had married a naval doctor and he was stationed at the base.

While at Worthy Down I did a one day 'catapult' training course at RNAS Gosport on Swordfish aircraft. To those of us who had been trained on Tiger Moths, the Swordfish was just like an overgrown Tiger Moth and equally easy to fly. After a short flight of

Proctor II

Lysander

20 minutes for 'experience on type', we were lifted by crane on to an old-type cordite-fired catapult and were hurled off into the air, which was quite hair raising. After four catapult take-offs, I was qualified for catapulting.

06/09/43 – 12/09/43

In September I went to RNAS Hinstock for an 'instrument flying course'. This was the naval advanced instrument flying school. We flew twin engined 'Oxford' aircraft with the cockpit 'hooded' so that all you could see were the instruments. This was very intensive and when not flying we were in the link trainer for hours. We then returned to Worthy Down.

This easy life at Worthy Down ended in early October 1943 when I was appointed to HMS Vulture, RNAS St Merryn in Cornwall, flying Seafires with 748 Squadron. A Seafire was the naval version of the Spitfire, with an arrester hook fitted for aircraft carrier landing, and with folding wings so that they can be stowed in the hanger deck.

07/10/43 – 06/12/43

This was a Seafire conversion unit based at St Merryn. I had my first flight in a Seafire on 15 October 1943, which was absolutely marvellous. We did a lot of squadron formation flying, air to air firing and splash firing into the sea. We did 'oxygen climbs' to 34,000 feet and dog fights at 20,000 feet.

We also did a lot of 'fighter affiliation' with all types of bombers from St Eval in Cornwall. This entailed our making dummy attacks on the bombers to train their gun crews. There was lots of aerobatics and low-level cross-country flying as well.

While at St Merryn, one evening a few of us visited the local Travose Head golf club where we met Prince Bira of Siam. I had watched him in the Ulster TT motor races on several occasions. His was a peculiar situation, in that he had been interned in the Isle of Man as an enemy alien until some of his racing pals got him out and, as he was an experienced pilot, got him a job as a Flying Officer in the ATC hidden away at Travose Head where he ran a gliding school training boys of the ATC. The day after we met him, he invited us up to his 'field' and we all had a go at his very basic glider, which was towed into the air by a winch mounted on the back of an old lorry. The 'field' was bordered on one side by high cliffs, so, once airborne, there was a great updraft from the wind hitting the cliffs.

RAF Chivenor, near Barnstable

Chivenor was more or less a continuation of the training we had been doing at St Merryn.

21/01/44

Towards the end of January 1944, I was drafted to HMS Landrail, RNAS Machrihanish, 772 Squadron, where I flew Martinet 1s which had Mercury XXX engines.

Machrihanish was a very cold and windy station. The first night Bertie Bassett and I were there, we were billeted in a nissen hut right down by the sea. In the middle of the night there was a severe gale and the hut literally took off, leaving us in our beds open to the weather. We made it up to the wardroom block in double quick time.

At Machrihanish we were asked to fly Rocs and Skua aircraft. We were not very keen on these two aircraft as they had a nasty habit of dropping the engine off on a heavy landing, so we spent days reading the handling notes. Our posting came just before we were going to be ordered to fly.

This posting to an operational squadron – 885 Squadron – was the one I had been waiting for all along.

On 12 February 1944 I left Machrihanish by Walrus, an amphibious aircraft which can land and take off from water or lower its wheels and operate from land. The weather conditions were very bad and after landing at Lamlash for a short wait we continued up the Clyde with the cloud base down to about 50 feet. We landed in the Clyde, lowered the wheels and taxied up the ramp at Greenock. Then by taxi to Glasgow and train to London and on to Portsmouth and Lee-on-Solent. I had arrived at an operational squadron at last.

Seafire

One of Prince Bira's gliders.

748 Squadron dispersal

Chapter 4
885 Royal Naval Air Squadron

The new 885 Squadron was forming at HMS Daedalus, Lee-on-Solent, to be equipped with Seafire Mk 111s and with 'Tiny' Devonald as CO. On arrival I was delighted to find that a lot of my friends from Worthy Down and Chivenor had also been posted to the same squadron.

On 19 February I collected my Seafire 111 from RNAS Burscough in Lancashire and flew back to Lee-on-Solent. By 21 February all 16 aircraft had been collected from all over England and the now complete Squadron formed up over Daedalus and set course in formation to St Merryn in Cornwall, known as HMS Vulture. Here we were to 'work up' for the forthcoming invasion.

During the first few weeks the training concentrated on formation flying and combat tactics. Then it switched to low-level navigation exercises over land and sea, which demanded highly accurate flying. The object was to prepare for 'fighter sweeps' with 2nd TAF (tactical air force).

CO 'Tiny' Devonald

On two occasions on these low-flying missions over the sea I very nearly had serious incidents. The first one was when a seagull hit my port wing during the early part of the flight. I continued and completed the mission and reported the 'bird strike' on landing. I was rather shaken when the engineer officer later reported that the main spar of the wing had been fractured and he did not understand how I had survived. On the second occasion it was another 'bird strike,' only this time in the radiator air intake. This was serious as the engine temperature immediately began to rise, so I set course for home and just made it before the engine seized. Of course that aircraft had to have a new engine fitted. As the Fleet Air Arm song goes: "Cracking show I'm alive / But I've still got to render my A25." The form A25 is a form which has to be completed when an aircraft has a 'prang' (crash) by the pilot, if alive, or by someone else if the pilot has not survived.

In mid March the Squadron Seafire 111s were exchanged for Seafire L111s. The 'L' signified 'low level', this version having clipped wing tips.

In the course of this exchange we had to fly our Seafire 111s up to Skebrae in the Orkneys. We left St Merryn in formation, landing at Machrihanish, very short of fuel, for lunch and refuelling.

We were sitting down for lunch in the wardroom and facing me was a row of fine looking 'Wren' stewards. As everyone around me had napkins and napkin rings I caught the eye of one of the Wrens opposite and tried to signal to her that I wanted a napkin. I held up my left hand forming a circle with my forefinger and thumb and passing the forefinger of my right hand in and out of the circle, to indicate to her that I required a napkin. To my terrible embarrassment a petty officer Wren came charging up to me accusing me of propositioning one of her Wrens.

After lunch, when I went back to my aircraft, I found one of the Wrens servicing my aircraft was an ex girlfriend of mine from Belfast. We only had time for a few words! I had given her up because I did not approve of her joining the Wrens

We then took off for Skebrae in very bad weather, again in formation. Climbing in 10/10ths cloud up a 'fiord' on the west coast, I became detached from the rest of the squadron. As I had no map, the CO carrying the only one, I did a 180 degree turn in the thick cloud and descended at the same rate of descent as we were using in the climb, and luckily emerged from the cloud at 500 feet between the two sides of the 'fiord.' I knew that the Caledonian Canal bisected Scotland, so I tried a few dead ends until I found it and flew up it with mountains on either side under a cloud base of 500 feet.

When I emerged at the other end of the canal, at Inverness, and started up the east coast, I realised I had to get a map or directions to Skebrae, so landed on a small grass airfield which turned out to be Fearne, an unused naval airfield only manned on a caretaker basis, so no maps were available. However, the caretaker officer was able to brief me round Wick, which was a heavily defended area, and report my position.

Having had no radio contact with the squadron, I was determined to get to Skebrae that day, as I assumed they were ahead of me. I took off, avoided Wick, flew past the 'Old Man of Hoy' and came to a low waterlogged island under a cloud base of about 100 feet. I got a fleeting glimpse of a runway, did a steep turn and landed. I did not know if I had found Skebrae or not, so, not wanting this to be known, I said to the sailor who climbed up unto my wing, "Have any of the others arrived yet?" He replied, "No Sir, you are the first." The weather was so bad that the rest of the squadron landed at Wick for the night and did not arrive at Skebrae until the next day.

From Skebrae we went to Hatston where all the 885 Squadron pilots, loaded down with their parachutes, Mae Wests and overnight bags, boarded a de Havilland DH 86, which is a four-engined biplane, for the trip back to St Merryn. This was nearly the end of us all because the pilot allowed one of our pilots to have a go flying this aircraft. Whatever he did, he got her into a spin so we had bodies, parachutes etc, flying all round the interior of the aircraft. Fortunately the pilot managed to regain control and pulled her out at about 100 feet above the Solway Firth. After this shake-up the engines were not running very smoothly so we had to land at

Boyd and Seafire

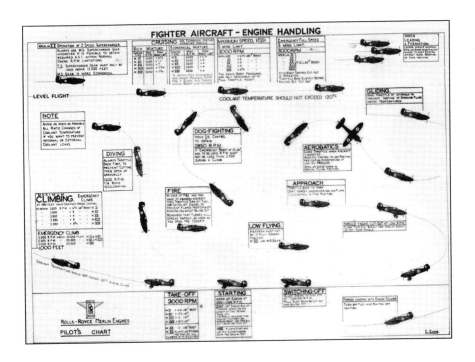

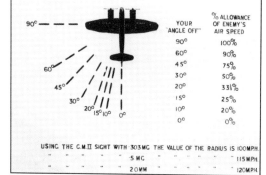

Seafires

Haverford West for a check.

Next day we took off again in the DH 86 for St Merryn. When we arrived, we found our new Seafire L111s had been flown in by ferry pilots, some very attractive girls amongst them!

This part of our 'working up' consisted of a lot of 'air firing'. The Seafire L111 carried an armament of two 20mm cannon and four machine guns of .303 inch calibre. We soon got used to the heavy recoil of the twin cannons which frequently shot the drogues clean away into the sea.

02/04/44 – 22/04/44

The month of April was spent at HMS Dipper at Henstridge in Somerset, mainly on low-level cross-country flying.

It came as a bit of a shock when instructions arrived on 20 April for the squadron to proceed to Scotland immediately, for a course in 'bombardment spotting'. Our task had changed, and now we would be controlling the gunfire of the Allied warships during the assault stage of the coming invasion of Europe.

22/04/44 – 06/05/44

On 22 April the squadron flew up to Dundonald in Ayrshire with a lunch and refuelling stop at Stretton. Dundonald was an RAF steel mesh airstrip, laid down on the second hole of the Royal Troon golf club. We were billeted a mile up the road at RAF Ayr.

Here we carried out 'bombardment spotting' exercises with various ships in the Firth of Clyde. The target area was the Isle of Arran. For 'bombardment spotting' we worked in pairs, one pilot doing the spotting while the other covered him. Height was important, 4,000 feet being the best, as it gave the pilot good surveillance and also kept the aircraft above the trajectory of the shells! The ship that I spotted for was mostly HMS *Enterprise* with her six-inch guns.

During a party at the end of the course we did 'the black footsteps' lark. This is where a pilot takes off his shoes and socks, blackens his feet from the back of the fireplace and, supported by his mates, walks up the wall and over the ceiling and down the wall on the other side, leaving a track of black foot prints. Unfortunately, on this occasion the pilot fell on a table and broke a lamp.

Next day the Group Captain of the station was furious and although we offered to pay for the small amount of damage he refused and demanded his pound of flesh, namely that our CO should produce a list of the three pilots responsible. The CO decided that all our names should be put in a hat, including his own, and that we should draw out three names. This happened and I was unfortunate to be one of the three. Long afterwards I learnt that I had lost six months seniority. A right twit that RAF Shylock was!

06/05/44 – 13/05/44

It was now off to RAF Heathfield for more 'spotting' practice with various ships.

On 13 May the squadron flew down to HMS Daedalus, refuelling at Burscough on the way. HMS Daedalus was to be our operational base for the invasion.

Our squadron was joined by 808, 886, and 897 Squadrons – all with Seafire L111s – to form No 3 Naval Fighter Wing. There were also two RAF Spitfire LVB squadrons and a US Navy squadron, the latter having recently converted from Kingfisher seaplanes to Spitfires.

The badge of No 3 Naval Fighter Wing.

All, like ourselves, were trained in bombardment spotting, and the entire group was under the command of 2nd TAF.

Certain changes in our aircraft were also taking place. As the Seafire had only a limited endurance, provision was made to fit a long-range fuel tank under the belly, with a release mechanism in the cockpit. The extra fuel would be used on the outward 'leg' of a mission, the tank then being jettisoned over enemy territory.

Another change was the replacement of the fixed-ring gunsight by the latest gyroscopic sight, which automatically applied the correct deflection without the pilot having to judge it. Also at this time we were all issued with 'G-suits'. These were like a rubber corset with legs. It was first laced up tightly and then filled with water after the pilot had strapped himself in the cockpit. Its purpose was to diminish the rush of blood from head to legs in manoeuvres involving heavy 'g' forces on the pilot, which normally caused a 'greying out' of the vision, and often a complete 'black out'.

At Lee, 885 Squadron had the good fortune to be billeted in a requisitioned house just outside the air station, the beach only a hundred yards away. We were very well looked after by four officers' stewards. Every few weeks we sent a lorry over to a brewery in Portsmouth for a barrel of best bitter to keep us cool in the hot weather.

On 2 June a complete security clamp-down was imposed, and all personnel were confined to their own bases, camps and marshalling areas, while full-scale briefings commenced

On 4 June we were surprised to find all our beautifully polished Seafires painted with wide bands of black and white paint on wing surfaces and around the fuselages. This was the war paint to adorn all Allied aircraft taking part in the coming operation, in order to eliminate any doubts about recognition. At Lee, columns of tanks and vehicles were parked nose to tail on the roads, whose crews slept and 'brewed up' on their vehicles.

The part to be played by HMS Daedalus was exactly as expected. No 3 Wing, with the attached RAF and USN squadrons, under the command of Commander 'Buster' Hallett, would commence spotting for the heavy guns of the Allied fleet at dawn on D-Day.

Chapter 5
Operation Overlord

D-Day

On 6 June 1944 I took off at 06.00 with Sub-Lt Rollins for our first sortie over the invasion beaches. The English Channel was an amazing sight, with thousands of ships of all sizes and shapes charging at full speed towards Normandy. On crossing the Normandy coast there was 10/10ths cloud at 2,000 feet and we throttled back and turned to coarse pitch just under the cloud base in order to drop our 'jet' tank. Suddenly, out of the cloud, diving flat out, was a Messerschmitt 109 coming at me head-on. He flicked to port and I flicked to port and we missed each other by a few feet.

We 'broke' (made a steep 180-degree turn) and started chasing him south, but had no chance of catching up. We then continued our patrol in the Trouville–Caen area, looking for impromptu targets for our ships. Finding none, we straffed and burnt two six-wheeled infantry carriers and a German motorcycle despatch rider. Before returning to Lee, I flew very low over Bertie Bassett's shot-down aircraft, believed to have been hit by 'flak' (anti-aircraft fire) on the Ouistraham golf club. He had been on the first sortie. His aircraft looked pretty well intact and I hoped he had got out and was making his escape, but this was not to be, as he was killed in the crash. He was a good friend and we had shared a room in the squadron house at Lee.

Sub-Lt AH Bassett RNVR.

Our second trip was after lunch when we were spotting for HMS *Ramilles*, reporting 'shoot not completed' and 'near misses' on an enemy battery.

Another pilot was also the victim of 'flak' and a third was

believed to have been blown up by a 16-inch shell from HMS *Nelson* while spotting at low level in bad visibility.

During the invasion the air traffic on the runway at Lee was so congested that we took off and landed in formation pairs. At any time there could be three pairs of Seafires on the runway at the same time.

During the first few days, in spite of our invasion markings, we were frequently being harassed by RAF Spitfires and US Lightnings swooping down on us to investigate, as, with our clipped wings, we could be mistaken for Me 109s. The assembled fleet was not much better.

So much for D-Day, what follows is a flavour of the scale of operations we undertook, and can be judged by the following extracts from my flying log book.

Next day, 7 June, we had three trips, the first two inconclusive, so we just straffed some transport. I felt that it was unfair to our marvellous riggers, fitters, armourers, and radio mechanics and all the other ground staff who worked tirelessly to keep us in the air not to have used our guns. So although we were not supposed to indulge in straffing, the troops back at our dispersal points at Lee expected to see the patches over the gun ports in the leading edge of our wings blown away and in tatters, which indicated to them that we had fired our guns. Also, being from around Comber, I concurred with the famous Ulster General Rollo Gillespie's battle cry "One more shot for the honour of Down."

On the third trip we had a shoot, with USS *Texas*, reporting targets hit. It was an amazing sensation flying a tiny Seafire fighter aircraft, whose air to ground fire power was very modest, and being able to bring down on a target such havoc from a ship's guns of up to 16-inch size.

Sadly, on 10 June, Reg, another of 885 Squadron's pilots, was shot down into the sea by a Canadian Spitfire pilot and was killed. On another occasion the 'boss', our CO, was attacked out of the sun by a Focke-Wulf 190, and his Seafire hit in the engine. He was last seen going down over the sea in a trail of smoke. For 24 hours there was

Year 1944		Aircraft		Pilot, or 1st Pilot	2nd Pilot, Pupil or Passenger Pair man	Duty (Including Results and Remarks)
Month	Date	Type	No.			
						Totals Brought Forward
June	3	Seafire LIIc	636	Self	—	Local Flying.
				Invasion.		
"	6	Seafire LIIIc	342	Self	S/Lt. Rollins	Patrol Trouville - Caen Area. No Impromptu Target Engaged. M.T. Engaged S.W. of Lisieux.
"	6	Seafire LIIc		Self	N.GR Rollins	Patrol Bayeux - Caen Area. Bombardment Spotting for Ramilles on Target 422107
"	7	Seafire LIIc	577	Self	Rollins	Dawn Take Off. Jet. Tank Lost over Solent.
"	7	Seafire LIIc	547	Self	Rollins.	Search for Impromptu Targets in W. Area nr Trevier. No Target Engaged.
"	7	Spitfire VB		Self	Rollins	Search for Impromptu Targets in W. Area. Bombardment Spotting for "Texas" at 661 801. Shoot not Completed.
"	12	Spitfire VB	3439	Self	Rollins	Bombardment Spotting for Nevada on Target 372 200 near Quettehou.
"	13	Seafire LIII	570	Self	Lt.Cdr. D.F.Vonald.	Lee to Thorny Island Squadron Formation.
				GRAND TOTAL [Cols. (1) to (10)]		

The author's log book entries for 6–13 June 1944.

no news of him, and we were beginning to fear the worst. Then he suddenly arrived in the Wardroom bar, with a plaster on his forehead, a big smile on his face, and an extra large thirst. 'Boss' had glided down and 'ditched' (landed in the sea) near one of our destroyers, but despite tight safety straps, the impact flung his head forward onto the bulky gyro gunsight, and he received a nasty gash on the brow.

On 12 June we spotted for USS *Nevada* on a target near Quettehou and reported straddles and hits obtained on two guns. On the way home we straffed some motor transport in a wood, again on my principle of "One more shot for the honour of Down."

My job was not always spotting, but varied according to

requirements. For example, on 13 June I flew with the CO as his No 2 to Thorney Island to pick up two Ansons and two Dakotas and escort them to landing strips at Bazenville and return. It was an uneventful passage; we were amazed that we came across so few German aircraft.

On 15 June we were again spotting for USS *Nevada*, reporting numerous hits in the target area, and on the second trip spotting for the same ship, reporting hits on two guns and installations. As they got more practice, the US ships were beginning to hit as many targets as the RN ships.

On 16 June most of the targets we were given had been eliminated and we were ordered to search for targets of opportunity in the Caen–Trouville area. There was no shoot as the ship's radio was unserviceable, but we found some rocket guns which we were able to pinpoint for the next flight. Then on 17 June we were spotting for a six-inch cruiser whose gunnery was lousy on two targets. Just after this we were 'jumped' (met) head on by three Me 109s. Our combined speed was such that we could not attack, so there was no combat and we returned to Lee very disappointed.

The second trip that day was a 'recce' (reconnaissance) of the west side of the Cherbourg peninsula, where it was reported that the Germans were evacuating the port along roads going south. By the time we got there, there were no targets left as the RAF had been there before us. The road south down the west side of the Cherbourg peninsula, as far as we could see, was just a mass of smoking and burning German transport, a beautiful sight! As it was not my policy to go home without firing my guns, I straffed a large group of Germans still holding out on the top of some cliffs near Cherbourg.

On 20 June we were again on a search for targets near Caen, but sea fog was obscuring everything so we had no targets.

The shoot of the invasion was on 23 June, when I operated with HMS *Erebus* and reported two very good shoots on factories and area targets. *Erebus* was a monitor and her shooting was so good that she really did not need 'spotters'. She would call me up and say "our target is the third bay of the factory on the right of the road running north and south through Ouistraham", and without any ranging shots she would hit her declared target each time with her first shot.

On 24 June I had a semi successful shoot at guns in a wood. On the way home I destroyed one lorry with 20 mm cannon. The trouble is that at this stage the targets were becoming very scarce.

On 25 June I had a shoot with USS *Quincey*, whose gunnery was poor and no targets were hit.

For a change from spotting on 29 June we flew as fighter escort to 20 Dakotas to a landing strip near Bayeux and returned without incident.

I had another change from the usual on 30 June when I flew a weather test for spotting near Caen.

On 5 July 'buzz bombs' began to appear. These were flying, unmanned jet-propelled small aircraft with bombs which flew across the channel until, their fuel exhausted, they glided down and exploded where they landed. They flew very fast and very low and were difficult to shoot down unless you had a large height advantage to dive on them with full throttle. I flew a 'buzz bomb' patrol over our base at Lee, but there was no alert during my time in the air.

Probably one of the most frightening things about the latter part of the invasion was sitting in a Seafire wearing a 'G' suit, strapped in and waiting instructions to start up, while the buzz bombs were passing over, never knowing if the buzz would stop or go on.

On 6 July a spotting mission east of Caen ended with no shoot as my radio was unserviceable. On the second trip the same thing happened – most annoying! Then the next day, 7 July, we were on buzz bomb patrol over base, but again there was no alert during my time in the air.

It was not all work, however. In the good weather, between

sorties, we would lie on the beach, which was only a few hundred yards from our house, with a good-looking Wren and enjoy the sun and try to relax. This was was not easy, as it was very difficult not to sit up and count the number of returning aircraft.

A new sortie, and a very frightening one, started on 8 July. This was an anti midget-submarine patrol ('goose hunt') off the British beaches. The Germans were supposed to have launched two-man midget submarines to attack the thousands of Allied ships anchored off the beaches

Our second trip was spotting south of Caen, which was nearly the end of us. Things seemed very quiet as we flew around Caen at about 3,000 feet with no sign of any flak, so we were careless and flew straight and level for a few minutes which was enough for the German gunners. When they got us on the far side of Caen they opened up with, it seemed, every gun in Caen. I got the fright of my life and immediately reacted as trained, by diving, climbing, ducking and turning to get clear, which we managed to do without damage. However, we had to abort the sortie due to this intensive accurate flack. It happened again the next day, 10 July; while spotting east of Caen we had to abort the sortie due to intense flack, this time from our guns along the River Orne.

Then it was back to anti midget-submarine patrol off the beaches on 11 July. These 'goose hunts,' as they were called, entailed flying as low as possible in and out of the ships moored off the beaches, most of which carried barrage balloons. During these hunts I never saw one midget submarine. Our second trip was another buzz bomb patrol over base, and again there were no alerts during my time in the air.

The following two final sorties from Lee are covered later: 12 July, Lee to Belfast ('Operation Strawberry'); 14 July, Belfast to Lee ('Operation Black Bush').

After our participation in Operation Overlord, 'Titch' Madden and I had the sad duty to perform of returning Bertie Bassett's car to his parents in Reading, as Bertie was now officially posted missing, presumed killed in action.

Also at this time we heard that Dave Cary – a very good friend of mine who had been a colleague on my original course – had been killed during the invasion of the south of France. He had been straffing a train in a cutting and had carried on his attack too long – he was not able to pull out and went straight into the train. He was an 'above average' pilot! Dave was a Canadian from Calgary and on several leaves I had brought him home with me to Whiterock where he was very popular with everyone.

During the early days of July, when Caen fell and the Cherbourg peninsula was liberated, the available gun and battery targets were beyond the range of our ships, so the 'bombardment spotting' operation from HMS Daedalus was finished. During this operation I had flown 30 missions as had most of the other pilots in No 3 Wing.

We were given weekend leave on 12 July which was insufficient for me to get to Belfast and back, so I took a chance and asked 'Buster' Hallett, No 3 Wing CO, if I could have my Seafire to fly to Belfast and back for the weekend. He agreed, much to my amazement, on the condition that I brought him back a case of 'Black Bush'.

At that time of the year the area round Lee-on-Solent was coming down with strawberries, so I unloaded the ammunition from all my guns except the two outer machine guns, just in case, filled the ammunition tanks with boxes of strawberries, and took off with bad weather forecast, determined to get home. When I got the length of somewhere around Chester, Air Control ordered me to land. I had to do a 'Nelson' and put my telescope to my deaf ear and proceeded.

I passed between the Calf of Man and the Island at zero feet in thick fog. I pulled up to about 1,000 feet to report my ETA (estimated time of arrival) at Sydenham in 10 minutes, got down to the deck again and flew up Strangford Lough, which I knew well, and 'beat up' the yachts sailing there, then up to 1,000 feet again and in to land at Sydenham. Mine was the first black and white striped aircraft, ie invasion aircraft, to land there which caused quite a stir.

I then got the cargo unloaded into a taxi, which took me to the bus station, where I got a bus to Ardmillan, near Killinchy. I had rung the local bank manager to meet me with his car, as he was the only person who had any petrol in those days. I rang Austin Boyd (no relation) of Old Bushmills Distillery and asked him for two cases of 'Black Bush,' duty free for the Navy, to be delivered to Sydenham first thing Monday morning. I reckoned the other pilots and I should have the second case.

After a hectic weekend I arrived at Sydenham expecting my aircraft to be fully refuelled, to find that they did not have the right nozzle, so we had to start refuelling with 50 gallon-drums and a funnel. While this was going on I carefully stowed the two cases of 'Black Bush' in the wing ammunition tanks.

An uneventful flight back to Lee followed, with the smoothest landing ever – not a single bottle broken!

No 3 Naval Fighter Wing – Summary of Operation Overlord

Enemy aircraft:	Destroyed, 2	Damaged, 5
Own aircraft:	Destroyed, 14	Damaged, 5
Pilots:	Killed, 4	
	Wounded, 2	
	Missing, 2	
Sorties flown:	Spotting, 993	
	Other, 237	
Hours flown:	2,510	

885 Squadron Casualties

Pilots:	Killed, 2 (Sub-Lts (A) Bassett and Kennett)
	Wounded, 1 (Lt (A) Metcalfe)

Chapter 6
Ulster

885 Squadron Re–formed

Soon after being 'stood down', 885 Squadron re-formed, losing some pilots, but gaining others from 886 Squadron, which was now disbanding.

The squadron was to move to the RAF station at Ballyhalbert, in Northern Ireland, prior to joining an aircraft carrier bound for the Far East. Ballyhalbert was a good station for me as I lived across Strangford Lough from Kircubbin, adjacent to Ballyhalbert.

I had a Ford 8 which I kept at my aircraft revetment (a three sided earth embankment where our aircraft were parked to protect them in the event of an air raid) and when my aircraft was refuelled by the 'bowser'(petrol tanker) they refuelled my car as well. It went like a bomb, with 100-octane fuel!

I kept a sailing boat at Kircubbin harbour so that I could take a few of my friends home by sea for dinner and drinks on many evenings. I also had the use of a 500cc squadron motorbike on which I did many runs up and down to Belfast.

Our dispersal area was right up against the perimeter fence and there was a pub, Bell's, on the other side, so, with the help of a pair of wire cutters, we had easy access. Most convenient.

'Working up' commenced all over again, as the squadron practiced fighter tactics and carried out endless ADDLs (airfield dummy deck landings) in preparation for carrier-borne operations.

One day, waiting in the queue for take off for ADDLs, I was stopped by a red Aldis lamp from the controller at the end of the runway. The aircraft behind me was too slow in applying his brakes and his propeller started chewing up my tail. I was out of the aircraft like a flash just before the FFI (Identification, Friend or Foe) blew up. It had a self-destruct device which blew it up in a crash so

Seafires of 885 Squadron over Strangford Lough, Co Down.

View from Kircubbin to Ballyhalbert airfield (centre top), Co Down.

that it would not fall into enemy hands.

However, that is not the end of that story. When my tail had been repaired, I had to do the test flight, and found that the aircraft would only turn to port no matter what I did. Scared stiff, I gently nursed her round in a very tight circuit and managed a safe landing. It transpired that the riggers or fitters had connected the control wires in reverse! Another very near shave!

One day when we were at Ballyhalbert there was an urgent call from RAFNI (Royal Air Force Northern Ireland) for some of our aircraft to bring down an unmanned American Flying Fortress which was heading for the Irish Free State. As we had no live ammunition at Ballyhalbert, my aircraft and another were loaded with 12 lb practice bombs and we were sent off to bring the Fortress down. I was not very keen about this, because if I had had to land in the Free State I would have been interned. The two of us found the Fortress and dropped our bombs from above without hitting it and returned to base. We heard that the Fortress over-flew Ireland and crashed in the Atlantic. The American crew had bailed out over England because of some minor fault in the aircraft.

At this time we had a practice bombing range at Kirkiston airfield, adjacent to Ballyhalbert. We also had a practice bombing range and skip bombing range at Gransha Point, a thin finger of land sticking out into Strangford Lough, south of Kircubbin.

At Gransha one of our training exercises was 'skip bombing' a line of old army vehicles. One day, on finishing my 'run' I heard a mayday call from the following pilot who had run into debris from the bomb dropped by the aircraft in front of him. It was a lovely sunny morning and I circled around the area until I saw his Seafire on the bottom, in very clear water off Monaghan Bank near Kircubbin. I am glad to say that the pilot was rescued but suffered a serious back injury and missed our Far Eastern operations.

Mention of these two ranges leads me to the story of the CO's court martial.

At that time there were all sorts of difficulties in travelling from

CO Tiny Devonald and Gwendoline.

England to Northern Ireland, and the CO had a girlfriend whom he wanted to bring over to be with him. So he organised a split-second timed operation. He picked Gwendoline up at Hawarden in a borrowed Auster aircraft and flew to Kirkiston, which was a small airfield just over the hill from Ballyhalbert, where I was organised to drive a Utilicon vehicle at speed alongside the landing Auster, while my helpers dragged Gwendoline from the Auster into the back of the Utilicon.

The CO took off again without stopping, flew over the hill and landed at Ballyhalbert, while my party took Gwendoline down to the Gransha Point range,where she was dressed as a Wren and mixed in with the other Wrens manning the range.

Eventually word got out about the whole affair and there was a civil prosecution at Greyabbey court. The night before the case, 885 Squadron pilots were entertained to a special dinner in Belfast by some leading businessmen, including my father. It so happened that the RM trying the CO's case was also a guest. The 'Boss' got off!

The Royal Navy, however, ordered him up to Eglinton, Londonderry, under house arrest until his court martial. Every morning while this lasted one of our pilots would fly up to Eglinton for some parts and have a good lunch and drinks with the CO to keep his spirits up.

He was dismissed his ship, but soon after got command of

Whiterock corner in 1944. The author's Whiterock family home is in the centre of the picture.

Bangor Golf Club, north Down.

Scrabo Tower, Newtownards, Co Down.

another squadron. He was awarded a DFC for 885 Squadron's bombardment spotting and other operations over Normandy.

At this time half the squadron went to Hawarden, near Chester, for PR (photographic reconnaissance) training. Whilst I was not in that half, I had a PR Spitfire to practice with at Ballyhalbert and photographed all the golf clubs, yacht clubs and friends' houses within range of Ballyhalbert. Taking further advantage of the squadron's division, a daily delivery of lobsters was made from Ballyhalbert to Hawarden.

Back on duty in dive bombing practice, one day I noticed that my Seafire had a small gap of about a quarter inch where the wings folded. I happened to mention this to the engineer officer in the bar that evening over a glass of beer. He got very agitated and asked me to go down to the revetment with him in his motor cycle and sidecar, equipped with torches etc, so that he could see for himself. On examining the wing-folding break, he decided to 'ground' all our Seafires. Whether it was due to this fault in the Seafires or for other reasons I do not know, but we were very soon re-equipped with Hellcat IIs.

My first flight in a Hellcat II was on 22 October. Compared to a Seafire it was like driving a double-decker bus after an MG sports car.

The hefty, rugged Hellcat, with its P & W twin bank, 18-cylinder, two-stage supercharged 45-litre 2000 Double Wasp radial engine, fitted with water injection for short bursts of even more power, was designed as a fighter-bomber for the US Navy. The cockpit was enormous after the petite, graceful Seafire. The armament consisted of six .5 inch machine guns, and with the addition of rocket rails, could carry eight rockets.

Once we were familiar with our new 'mounts' they were very nice to fly. The advantages of the Hellcat over the Seafire were immediately apparent. In the tail down attitude, the short nose allowed a better view forward, and the robust undercarriage reduced the risk of damage from a heavy landing.

We now had to put in a lot of ADDLs (airfield dummy deck

landings) as we were due to embark in a newly commissioned aircraft carrier, HMS *Ruler*, in seven weeks time. All these ADDLs seemed very boring (at this point my Log Book showed 678 hours flying completed) but certainly proved their worth when it came to the real thing. That's why I am able to write this story.

We continued 'working up' with dive bombing, skip bombing and rocket firing. The rocket firing range was an island close to the shore, just north of Kircubbin. On one occasion, after I had fired my first two rockets and was pulling out of my dive, I partially blacked out and my hand slid up the stick and touched the firing button sending another two rockets up into the sky towards Kircubbin. Fortunately they landed in the sea just outside the harbour.

On 15 December we flew our aircraft to RNAS Sydenham, folded our wings and taxied to the airport wharf where HMS *Ruler* was alongside. Our aircraft were hoisted on board while we walked up the gangway to join our new home. We all immediately went down to the wardroom still in our flying clothes. I had a Red Hand of Ulster emblem stitched on to the front of my Mae West and when one of *Ruler*'s officers saw this he jumped up and came over and introduced himself as a 'towney' (someone from the same town). This was Lt John Robson, RNR. I was to see a lot of him from then on!

There is an interesting story about my Red Hand emblem. It had been sent to an uncle, after whom I was named 'George,' when he was selected to play rugby for Ulster during World War One. He was a doctor and, having joined the army, he was posted to German East Africa before he could play. Sadly he died there a short time later.

Our stay in Ulster was most enjoyable, with many trips to the Officers Club in Belfast and such places. Before we left Belfast one of our pilots, Harry Simpson, and his fiancee, Betty, a WAAF from Ballyhalbert, got married on 6 January in St Anne's Cathedral. (There was no long-term planning here – in wartime, we took the opportunities as they came.) They were still married in 2000 when, sadly, Harry died. He was a very decent Englishman and used to annoy me when we were flying together by using, as a joke, the callsign 'Fenian 1' for him and 'Fenian 2' for me.

885 Squadron re-equipped with Hellcats. Four of the eight rocket mounts are clearly visible under the wing.

Hellcats

Boyd

Chapter 7
HMS *Ruler*

HMS *Ruler* was one of the many American escort carriers in service with the Fleet Air Arm, acquired under 'lend-lease' arrangements. Her flight deck was only 460 feet long. Her maximum speed was 17–18 knots, which was barely enough for a Hellcat to make a normal take-off. Some wind speed was also required. With sufficient wind and full power the Hellcat would be airborne just forward of the bridge and be raising its undercarriage before crossing the bow. If there was not sufficient wind over the deck, the aircraft had to be launched by catapult (usually called the accelerator). The accelerator was located on the forward port side of the flight deck, and could accelerate a Hellcat, with its engine at full power, from a standing start to a flying speed of about 80 knots in 30 yards. It was cable-operated by a large hydraulic single-cylinder drive five decks below. The wire rope connecting it to the aircraft towing hook had a 91-foot run on deck and the speed achieved by the hook alone was about 60 knots, the propeller contributing a further 10 to 20 knots, giving a speed well above stalling speed. With experienced flight deck handling and catapult parties, aircraft could be catapulted at two-minute intervals.

Stretched across *Ruler*'s flight deck were nine arrester wires and three barriers. The arrester wires and barriers were each connected to a plunger in a cylinder filled with a special fluid, located athwartships under the flight deck. The plunger had valves which allowed the fluid to pass through and thus stop the aircraft at a comfortable rate, I usually managed to pick up number 3 wire. To float until Nos 7 or 8 or worse still, No 9 wire was picked up (especially in a too fast approach) would risk a tussle with one of the barriers, with damaging results. After an arrester wire was hooked on touch down, it was drawn out with increasing resistance, until the aircraft came to a halt in about 100 feet or more, throwing the pilot forward against his restraint straps. During landing, two barriers were raised as an arrest of last resort, in case an arrester hook broke or bounced over all the wires, or the pilot floated too far forward on the deck. After the barriers were lowered, an aircraft had its wings folded and was taxied beyond the barriers where it could be parked or taken below on the lift to the hanger. There were two lifts, one forward and another aft.

The ship's officers were mainly RNVR, with a sprinkling of RN who had no previous experience of aircraft carriers. *Ruler* put to sea on 19 December, and steamed into the Firth of Clyde for the first deck-landing practice. Flying went very smoothly at first, but after about 30 deck landings by several pilots, Sub-Lt (A) Dick Goadsby caught his arrester hook on the round-down and ended up at high speed in the barrier. The aircraft was a 'write off'. On Christmas Eve, after another 100 or so uneventful landings, Sub-Lt (A) George Horne also broke off his hook, ended up on his nose with a bent engine, and another Hellcat had to be sent ashore and replaced.

'Working up' continued until 18 January, by which time I had done nine deck landings.

During three weeks of flying training from *Ruler* there were heavy rainstorms and some thick fog in the Firth and, when necessary, the ship's Fighter Direction staff were prompt in diverting those who were airborne to RNAS Ayr. Out of about another 400 deck landings, there were half a dozen more incidents, including one spectacular one on 27 December when two Hellcats were lost. Sub-Lt Mike Furnival approached the deck through a rain squall, bounced over the barriers, and crashed into Lt (A) Sam Lang's aircraft parked forward, from which he had just leaped out into the port catwalk. Both Hellcats careered overboard in great balls of flame and plunged into the sea in a cloud of steam, from which Sub-Lt Furnival swam out of his cockpit and was recovered by the attendant escort.

Sub-Lt (A) Jim Fisher left us in the Clyde. In his deck landing approach, he was seen to stall directly into the sea astern of the ship from about 200 feet. He was rescued, but severely damaged his spine and was subsequently invalided out of the Service.

HMS Ruler

An early draft of a badge for HMS Ruler. *See Appendix VI for its final form (page 115).*

At night *Ruler* either dropped anchor off Lamlash or swung to a buoy in Rothesay Bay, on the Isle of Bute. We had frequent 'runs' ashore, always being well received by the locals, both in their pubs and at their village dances.

As a change from normal take-offs, we were occasionally launched into the air by catapult (really a compressed air accelerator). This was a convenient and efficient way of dispatching individual aircraft, without having to turn the ship into wind.

Deck landings soon became routine, but the risks were always greater than airfield landings, and occasional mishaps had to be expected. Following every flying accident, form A25 had to be completed by the pilot (if alive). Over the years, this form filling solemnity had given rise to the Fleet Air Arm's most legendary song – 'The A 25.' There were many verses, commenting satirically on a variety of hazardous and amusing flying situations, the general tone being both bawdy and irreverent. In 885 Squadron we had learned the song earlier from the 'Boss', our CO at the time of the Invasion. Now that we were at sea, and inevitably experiencing our share of mishaps, the lines of this ballad took on a new reality.

The chorus went 'Cracking show I'm alive! / But I've still got to render my A25!' If the Fleet Air Arm has a hymn (although that is not quite the correct term) it is 'The A25'. To continue:

> They say in the Air Force a landing's okay,
> If the pilot gets out and can still walk away,
> But in the Fleet Air Arm the prospects are dim,
> If the landing's piss poor and the pilot can't swim.
>
> Chorus:
> Cracking show, I'm alive,
> But I've still got to render my A25.
>
> I fly for a living, and not just for fun,
> I'm not awfully anxious to hack down the Hun,

And as for deck landings at night in the dark,
As I told Wings this morning, '____ that for a lark.'
Chorus

When the batsman gives 'Lower' I always go higher,
I drift off to starboard and prang my Seafire,
The boys in the Goofers all think that I'm green,
But I get my commission from Supermarine.

Chorus

I thought I was coming in low enough but,
I was fifty feet up when the batsman gave 'Cut',
And loud in my earholes the sweet angels sang,
Float, float, float, float, float, float . . . Barrier . . . PRANG!

Chorus

They gave me a Seafire to beat up the Fleet,
I beat up the Nelson and Rodney a treat,
But then I forgot the high mast on Formid,
And a seat in the Goofers was worth fifty quid.

Chorus

from *The Fleet Air Arm Song Book* (tune: 'Villikins and his Dinah')

By 20 January, the flight deck and hanger were filled with Hellcats, Corsairs and Avengers as well as the Fireflies of 1772 Squadron, whose aircrews and maintenance team came aboard as passengers, and severely crowded the living spaces.

On 21 January Sub-Lts Dowsett, Napier, Orr and CPO Moncur joined the squadron in Belfast. To the CO's consternation, although the four new arrivals had flown the smaller Wildcat, none had flown the much more powerful Hellcat before, and they were too late for the squadron's operational sea training off the UK. As it happened, all four of those pilots suffered major accidents while

A 'prang' on board HMS Ruler.

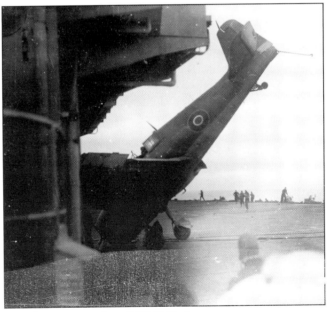

Another prang on board HMS Ruler.

with 885, either while training in Australia or on the Pacific operations. Most sadly, two of them were fatal.

One of the great advantages of being at sea was that every month my father was able to send me 2,000 duty free cigarettes from Gallaher's tobacco factory. The collection of mail on *Ruler* was very erratic. Sometimes I had no smokes for weeks and then two or three parcels would arrive. I was very popular on those occasions!

On 28 January 1945, in company with HMS *Activity*, we left Greenock to join the Eastern Fleet. Our hanger and flight deck were filled to capacity with aircraft. In addition to our own Hellcats, we carried replacement Avengers and Corsairs, hence there could be no flying until we reached our destination, wherever that was!

With no flying possible the squadron pilots assembled in the briefing room every morning for lectures and films, the latter mainly instructional. The most popular film was *Heavenly Body*, featuring Hedy Lamarr.

In addition to normal squadron administrative duties (I was the squadron armament officer) we had to understudy the ship's officers. I became second navigation officer under John Robson. In addition to that I was on the roster for 2nd officer-of-the-watch (OOW).

Ruler joined a Gibraltar-bound convoy which was screened by an escort of destroyers and corvettes. As the convoy ploughed its way through the Bay of Biscay, *Ruler* was being pounded by heavy seas, pitching, rolling and juddering continuously, which ensured plenty of vacant places at table in the wardroom. After a short stop at Gibraltar, we left the convoy and proceeded eastward unescorted. Things seemed to be going well and I was doing a lot of the navigation, under John's watchful eye of course, when we ran into a vicious storm south of Sardinia. The ship was forced to slow down for a few hours, for the safety of the aircraft lashed down on the flight deck.

During this storm the seas had lifted the forward end of the flight deck, so we now went into Alexandria for repairs. We were there for nearly a week, so all had a good time ashore. We played rugby at the sporting club before King Faruk and dined at the famous Pastroudi's. During our stay, apparently, Roosevelt and Churchill arrived from the Yalta conference aboard a US battleship and Churchill transferred to the *Newfoundland*.

Ruler then steamed past Port Said and into the Suez Canal. The journey down the 100-mile length of the canal was tediously slow. After a stop in the Bitter Lakes to allow a north-bound convoy to clear the lower half of the Canal, we continued. We eventually cleared Suez, and headed for the open waters of the Red Sea.

Schools of porpoises came on the scene eager to act as escorts and kept station alongside the ship for miles. The weather now became really hot, but we had to be very careful not to get sunburn as it was a punishable offence to become unfit for duty for this reason. In the Indian Ocean we were beset by schools of flying fish for days, some landing on the sponsons (platforms projecting from the ship's side) but not quite making the flight deck.

On 27 February 1945 we arrived in Colombo, Ceylon (now Sri Lanka). During the three days we spent there, we swam in the sea at Mount Livinia and dined at the Galle Face Hotel and did some shopping. The visit to the Galle Face Hotel was the only occasion when I had the opportunity to wear my 'Number 10s.' Number10s are white suits buttoned right up to the neck, like a barber's jacket, and most uncomfortable in the heat – typical old-fashioned and inefficient naval garb. In Colombo harbour was a hospital ship, some of whose nurses we met; they were all terrific lookers.

When 885's Hellcats were first loaded on board *Ruler*, in December 1944, they were all painted in matt dark brown and green RN European theatre camouflage, with red and blue roundels. Replacements were received in Belfast with the USN's Pacific blue gloss finish, which was much easier to clean and did not bleach, as the European colours did in the tropics. An Admiralty fleet order (AFO) required that the roundels be changed to blue and white (to eliminate the Japanese red) in Eastern Fleet insignia. Another AFO was received requiring RN aircraft in the Pacific area of operations to have USN-style markings. They were fairly similar to the USN's

The deck cargo en route to Australia.

HMS Ruler *passing through the Suez Canal.*

Suez landscapes.

star and bars design, had to be devoid of red as in the Japanese insignia, and had to have a most distinctive large white and blue roundel, easily seen from some distance away.

On 1 March we left Colombo bound for Sydney, Australia, a distance of 4,500 miles. As was customary, *Ruler* held a 'crossing-the-line' ceremony for those of us, myself included, who had not crossed the Equator before. Then it was on again along the southern coast of Australia, eventually reaching our journey's end, Sydney, on 16 March 1945.

The 'crossing-the-line' ceremony of 'King Neptune's court' on board HMS Ruler *on 4 March 1945 – the author's twenty-second birthday.*

Chapter 8
Australia

Ruler steamed through the 'Heads' into Sydney's marvellous harbour on 16 March 1945. We slid under the majestic bridge and entered the docks area where we tied up alongside Pyrmount No 12 dock. Our deck cargo of aircraft were unloaded and transferred by road to Mascot airport, ready to be flown aboard carriers returning from the north with depleted squadrons. We had a terrific party to celebrate our arrival and St Patrick's Day. With her flight deck clear again *Ruler* put to sea on 18 March and 885 Squadron flew off to MONAB 3 at Schofields, on the outskirts of Sydney. We did not actually fly off – we were catapulted off, and therein lies a hair-raising story.

I had just started up my engine and moved up to the catapult and had been attached to it, when, before I had run up my engine or applied full throttle, someone pressed the 'tit' and I was catapulted off with my engine idling. The normal procedure is that once the pilot is attached to the catapult he opens the throttle to full and tightens a friction nut so that it can't slip back, puts his head tightly against the head cushion to prevent 'whiplash effect' which could break his neck, and when ready raises his hand to face level and then drops it, which is the signal for the catapult to be fired.

In spite of the previous night's party, my reactions were swift. In one movement I had selected wheels up and full throttle, I then nursed my sturdy steed on in a shower of spray before she began to lift a little, and then, with engine firing well at last, I was able to fly on to Schofields (HMS Nabthorpe). Although our Hellcats were fitted with a water injection system, it was not meant to be used with salt water!

On landing I was handed a signal from *Ruler*'s Captain apologising for what had happened and congratulating me on my survival.

HMS Ruler *arriving in Sydney, 16 March 1945.*

Pyrmount No 12 dock, Sydney. HMS Ruler *is forward of HMS* Fencer *with both of her aircraft lifts down.*

Schofields airfield, near Sydney.

Pilots at Schofields. The author is pictured fifth from left.

Another pilot, Sub-Lt Hardwick, was not as fortunate as I and went into the drink, but I am glad to say he was picked up by our rescue escort.

Schofields was a 'MONAB,' which stood for mobile naval air base, of which there were a number in the Far Eastern theatre. Each was a completely self-contained unit, having the necessary equipment to clear and level a suitable area of ground, and lay a steel mesh airstrip.

At Schofields we started to 'work up' again after a lay-off of two months. Being airborne was strange at first, but it is like riding a bicycle – you never forget.

The hospitality of the people of Sydney was superb just as it had been in Canada. We were inundated with invitations and many firm friendships developed with families and individuals, some of whom took us out sailing in the harbour and swimming at Bondi Beach and Manly Beach. We were also made temporary members of the Imperial Services Club, which was a great honour. Many a good evening was spent here.

The licensing laws were rather strange in Australia, as the pubs only opened for an hour from 6 o'clock to 7 o'clock. This meant that they had huge long bars with dozens of barmen pulling 'schooners' (pints) of beer for the crowds of customers as fast as they could. By the end of the hour they were all 'full' – not our leisurely way of having a pint! We spent many happy evenings in restaurants and night clubs such as Romano's, which was very popular.

On 9 April we flew down to Jervis Bay to land on *Ruler* again, and to carry out three days of deck landing practice. After two months 'off' flying, during the passage to Australia, doing our mundane ship's duties, it was a rather terrifying thought to have to start deck landings again. Our original deck landing training had taken place in the Clyde and here we were in the southern hemisphere starting it al lover again.The Hellcat, with its wide stable undercarriage and good forward view was a beautiful aircraft to deck land, but it was always a very 'dicey' business getting down onto what looked like an elongated postage stamp when viewed from 2,000 feet. The Hellcat's maximum take off weight of 15,000 lbs was more than double that of a Seafire. In calm weather deck landing was not too bad, but in heavy seas with the ship pitching and rolling violently, it was a very scary job.

During our deck landing training at Jervis Bay we carried a reporter from the *Sydney Daily Telegraph*, and the following is his report of 26 March 1945:

> If half a dozen planes come in successfully without one getting a 'wave off' from the signalman you are doing pretty well; for landing on the deck of a small carrier in a rough seas is just about like landing on half a block in Main Street while a combined hurricane and earthquake is going on.
>
> You would call it a perfect landing if the plane came in and hit both wheels at the same time in the centre of the deck, headed straight forward and caught about the third of one of the cables stretched across the deck.
>
> But few of them are perfect. They come in in a thousand different ways. If their approach is too bad the signalman, waves them round again.
>
> They will sometimes come in too fast, and hit the deck so hard that a tyre blows. They will come in half sideways and the cable will jerk them round in a tyre screeching circle. They will come in too close to the edge of the deck and sometimes go right over the catwalk. They will come in so high that they miss all the arrester gear and slam into the high cables stretched across the mid deck called the barrier.
>
> Sometimes they do a somersault over the barrier and land on their backs. Sometimes they bounce all round and hit the island. Sometimes they bounce 50 feet into the air and still get down alright. Sometimes they catch fire.
>
> And on the other hand they will land planes for weeks without a bad crack up . . . IT'S NO CIRCUS !

Hellcats on the 'round down'.

A Hellcat awaiting take-off from the catapult.

While at Jervis Bay one of our Hellcats broke his arrester hook on the 'rounddown' (the stern of the flight deck) and went into the barrier. The aircraft was a 'write off.'

Here we also had some 1772 Squadron Firefly crews for deck landing training. Three of them took off and, on landing back on, all three crashed. These were Australian pilots who had not had sufficient training. All three aircraft had to be 'ditched'. I should explain that operational squadrons were numbered in the 800s and the 1700s and training squadrons in the 700s.

I had a very close call one day doing a low-level cross-country in Australia. I was flying up a river at about twenty feet when I suddenly saw high-tension cables straddling the river. In the split second I had to decide to go over or under. I went under. When I landed it was quite a relief to see that there were no cables dangling from my tailplane!

After our very pleasant Australian stay *Ruler* was sent northwards to join the British Pacific Fleet, renamed by the Americans as Task Force 57. We were to travel with the 'fleet train' and provide CAP (combat air patrol) over the fleet when it was refuelling and replenishing from the fleet train.

My job as 885 squadron armament officer on the way up the east coast of Australia was to 'harmonise' all our Hellcat guns. This entailed setting up a design of roundels (large targets or dartboards) on the raised barrier, jacking up the tail of the aircraft to a flying position at the stern of the flight deck, removing the bolts from the guns, and, with a periscope, looking down the barrels and adjusting the guns on to the roundels one by one (8 guns per aircraft) so that when fired the bullets from all eight guns would converge at the same point say 200 yards ahead of the aircraft and cause most damage to the enemy aircraft. I spent most of the daylight hours scrambling over the wings, being buffeted by the slipstream from the ship's forward movement.

While *Ruler* was steaming at best possible speed along the north coast of New Guinea, part of which was still held by the Japanese, a

Hellcat was ranged on the catapult just in case. We again had a small deck cargo so could not fly off in the normal way.

We proceeded through the Coral Sea, along the coasts of Papua New Guinea, and on 24 April *Ruler* entered the anchorage at Leyte, in the Philippine Islands, which had just recently been liberated by the Americans. Here lay the British task force, a most impressive gathering of modern sea power, with four 'fleet' carriers, two battleships of the King George V class, and dozens of heavy and light cruisers, destroyers and submarines.

Two days after arriving in Leyte Bay ten of our pilots were transferred by boat from HMS *Ruler* to the 'fleet' carrier HMS *Indomitable*. They were joining another Hellcat squadron, 1844, to replace pilots lost in action, and those now due for a rest.

During the next few months we called in to Manus, our forward base in the Admiralty Islands, and on our first visit there I met some US naval pilots who told me of all the equipment they had and we did not, including survival kits. So, as the survival officer of our squadron, and with the Americans' generous help, I managed to produce kits for our pilots which we wore on our backs. However when we were passing Papua New Guinea and Borneo, where cannibals were located, I did not add the cloth sheet the Americans had given me which had the following message printed in broken Aussie/Pacific language "If you hand this fellow to either of the nearest US or British base you will be rewarded with $100. Do not eat him." I thought that the cannibals would not be able to read anyway!

During the next few months there were many 'prangs'(crashes) on deck; if the aircraft could not be immediately repaired it was pushed over the side of the ship. Sometimes there was time to salvage bits and pieces from the aircraft before pushing it over. In this way I managed to salvage a 20mm Hispano Swiza cannon and had it boxed as new in case I could sell it to someone. But no luck. I also salvaged a cine camera but unfortunately it was 24 volts, which was not much good when I finally got back home.

The photograph section of the ship came under the squadron armament officer so, while on board, I had a good supply of film for my ancient, large, folding Kodak camera.

Pilots of 885 Squadron on board HMS Ruler, Indian Ocean, February 1944.

Back row (L–R): Sub-Lts R Hales, G Boyd, Lt J Bowles, Sub-Lts G Horne, M Furnival, Lts B Tucker, D Tugby, Sub-Lt A Taylor.

Middle row: Sub-Lts H Napier, G Bantham, Lt H Simpson, Lt-Cmdr J Routley (CO), Lts S Lang, D Papworth, Sub-Lts D Lewis, W Woodfield.

Front row: Lt T Handley, Sub-Lts K Coulthurst, D Hartland, J Vercoe, R Thomas, L Dowsett, B Chamen.

Also: Lt M Brooshooft and Sub-Lt R Goadsby (watch keeping).

Chapter 9
Pacific

Operation Iceberg II

On 29 April the Task Force sailed from Leyte heading for the 'Area Cootie'. This was the area on the chart where the fleet train cruised up and down while the fleet went on their operations and returned to refuel and replenish from the fleet train. We sailed from Leyte on 3 May and while the Air Group were attacking airfields in Sakishima Gunto, we were flying CAP over the 'fleet train.' We reached the replenishment area on 5 May. This pattern continued through the month of May. Combat air patrol, at least in the case of *Ruler*'s pilots, was a most tedious duty. Two aircraft took off from *Ruler* and patrolled over the 'fleet train' for two to three hours, flying back and forth over the ships and seeing no intruders. Flying in the Pacific was very different from flying in Europe as, on a CAP, you could find yourself over 200 miles away from the carrier in the middle of the Pacific Ocean and unable to reach land, hostile or otherwise, in any direction. The ship had a 'beacon' which sent out radio signals in segments with a different morse letter in each segment, so that if you were flying in on the letter A and it turned to the letter B you knew that you had gone too far in that segment and altered course accordingly. This beacon worked as long as you were in range, say about 150 miles from the ship. On most days during the month of May 1945 I flew two CAPs per day, and in that month a total of 45 hours.

On 6 May the fleet returned to refuel and replenish from the RFAs (royal fleet auxiliaries) *Wave King, Wave Monarch, San Ambrosia, San Adolpho and Cedardale*, escorted by the destroyers *Napier, Norman and Nepal*, the escort carriers *Striker* and *Ruler*, and the escort vessels *Crane, Avon, Whimbrel* and *Pheasant*. The fleet (large) carriers *Indomitable, Indefatigable, Victorious and Formidable*, and the battleships *King George V* and *Howe*, and countless cruisers, destroyers and other

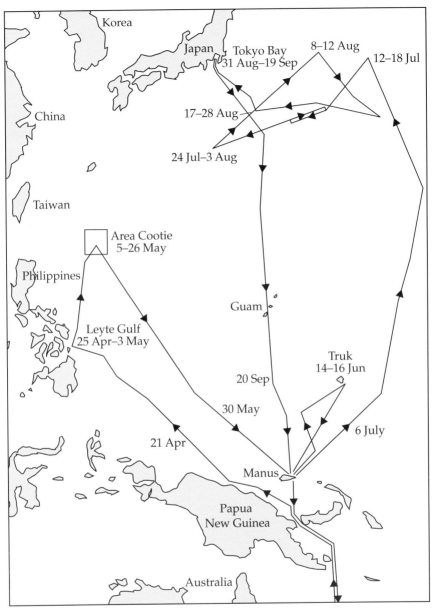

Map of HMS Ruler's *passages in the Pacific for all operations, including those off Japan.*

A Fleet Train tanker refuelling two destroyers abeam by the USN method and HMS Ruler *by a buoyant hose streamed astern.*

Sub-Lt (A) Les Dowsett returning to HMS Ruler *via 'breeches buoy' from HMS* Queenborough *after ditching in the Pacific.*

'escort' carriers rejoined us from time to time for refuelling etc.

On 8 May the news of the German unconditional surrender and the deaths of Hitler and Goebbels were received and we 'spliced the main brace'. A very convivial evening was had, but we were still very much at war in the Pacific and became the 'forgotten fleet' as far as the UK was concerned.

At this point it might be well to explain that all the Allied ships were being attacked by Japanese kamikaze pilots and the American carriers, having wooden decks, suffered severely, whereas all our 'fleet' carriers had armour plated decks through which the kamikazes could not penetrate. A kamikaze could dive on to an American carrier, open up the flight deck and go right through into the hanger space below, which would normally put an American carrier out of action. *Ruler*, being American built, had the usual wooden deck, but luckily we never saw a kamikaze. Kamikaze was the name which the Japanese navy gave to its suicide pilots. The name itself meant 'divine wind'.

We had a mishap on 10 May when Sub-Lt (A) Dowsett ditched on take off in a Hellcat, apparently because he had his 'airscrew' in coarse pitch when it should have been in 'fine' pitch for take-off. Luckily he was picked up by our escort destroyer and returned to *Ruler* by 'breeches buoy'. Again, on 15 May, Sub-Lt Bowles had to ditch on take off and was picked up and returned to *Ruler*.

On 10 May the fleet rejoined our fuelling force, comprising the tankers *Arndale*, *Dingledale* and *San Amado*, with the *Aase Maersk*, the tug *Weasel*, the *Whylla*, *Bal-Carat*, the *Crane*, the *Pheasant* and *Nepal*. Fuelling was completed on the afternoon of the 11 May and the 'fleet' took its departure on 15 May. On 18 May and 19 May, we were again with the 'fleet' for refuelling and replenishment.

At dawn on 20 May, in heavy fog, the destroyer *Quilliam* collided heavily with the carrier *Indomitable*. 'Indom' suffered slight damage to her stern, but the destroyer had her bow crumpled and bent backwards. Another destroyer, *Norman*, took her in tow, but was not making much of it, so the tug *Weasel* had a go and then the cruiser

Black Prince. During this operation *Ruler* provided air cover.

We had a tragedy on 23 May when Sub-Lt (A) Horace Napier took off in coarse pitch, did not gain sufficient flying speed, and flew into the sea off the starboard bow. He was unable to get out of his cockpit and sank with his Hellcat without resurfacing.

Emergency Landing

Shortly after take-off on one of my CAPs I was half asphyxiated and blinded by a spray of hydraulic fluid in the cockpit so I had to get down again as soon as possible. This was difficult as, after my flight had taken off, *Ruler* had altered course to stay with the fleet train; to take me on again would mean she would have to alter course into wind and and away from the protection of the fleet train's destroyer screen, making herself vulnerable to submarine attack. I was ordered to bail out or ditch! I was not very happy about either so I did a deal over the radio that *Ruler* would turn into wind and give me ONE chance to land, otherwise I would ditch.

I managed the landing! I was pretty well unconscious from the fumes, but my CPO armourer got me out of the cockpit and down to his mess where he gave me a few large glasses of 'neaters' (undiluted naval rum), which soon revived me. Then, over the tannoy, came the insistent message 'Sub Lt Boyd report to the bridge immediately'.

With the help of my faithful CPO armourer I managed to find the bridge and report to the Captain, who was dressed in immaculate 'whites,' while I was dressed in rough flying clothes covered in oil etc. To my amazement he congratulated me on my landing and dismissed me.

I should admit that one of the reasons I did not want either to parachute or to ditch was that shortly before I had taken off, a Corsair pilot had had to ditch quite close alongside the ship. He had survived the ditching and had inflated and boarded his rubber dinghy and, although he was picked up very quickly by a boat from our escort, he was violently seasick during his time in his rubber dinghy. I was proud of the fact that I had never been seasick during

'Bowles Centenary' celebration for Sub-Lt (A) Bowles on HMS Ruler. He had made his 100th deck-landing during Operation Iceberg II, May 1945.

Hellcat 'prang' after its hook was pulled out on the stern of the flight deck, resulting in the aircraft being unable to pick up an arrestor wire before hitting the barriers.

Ponam Island airfield on the small coral island off Manus in the Admiralty Islands, June 1945.

Ponam 'heads' (loos).

Ponam Island cinema.

this trip and did not want to risk it in a rubber dinghy.

One day I was on the bridge taking the 'noon sight' with a sextant (a navigational instrument) while aircraft were landing, when there was a loud bang and a Hellcat wing spiralled through my sight to land in the sea to starboard. It gave me quite a fright. In this 'prang' I am sorry to say the pilot, Peter Orr, went over the bow and he and Grant (the pilot of the Avenger he landed on) were both killed.

This was a very busy time for the *Ruler* pilots. The CAP flights lasted approximately two and a half hours and often I flew two CAPs in a day. One day we had two pilots who 'went in' on take-off apparently because they were in coarse pitch instead of in fine pitch, ('pitch' means the angle of the propeller blades.) Only one managed to get out and was recovered by our escorting corvette.

Several times *Ruler*'s deck was fouled by 'prangs' so I had to land on other carriers: *Victorious*, *Speaker*, *Chaser* and *Arbiter*. The day I had to land on *Victorious* was shortly after she had had a kamikaze strike and the deck was a mess. I was on board for a few hours before I could go back to *Ruler*, during which time one of their surgeon lieutenants offered me the thumb of the kamikaze pilot in a bottle of formaldehyde as a souvenir.

On some occasions we pilots were transferred from one carrier to another by destroyer and breeches buoy, which can be a tricky business in high seas. However, I survived that as well. Between 6 May and 28 May I flew 19 combat air patrols and never saw a Jap aircraft.

At the beginning of June the fleet withdrew to Sydney for action damage repairs and for leave, while we went to Manus in the Admiralty Islands where we were to do dummy kamikaze attacks on the ships in Manus. *Ruler*'s pilots rebelled at this as 885 Squadron pilots had done more flying hours than the fleet pilots and also deserved leave. Luckily the Captain took our side, gave us a week's leave, and a Dakota was organised to fly us from Monote (Admiralty Islands) down to Sydney, landing at Lae (New Guinea), Milne Bay, Townsville (North Queensland), Archer Field (Brisbane) and finally Mascot (Sydney).

We had a great week in Sydney; it rained all the time!

We then went back up to Manus again. On arrival back on *Ruler* we were immediately sent by landing craft to Ponam Island on 20 June. Ponam was a small coral island north of Manus, with the usual lagoon enclosed by an outer ring of coral reef. It was very hot, so much so that one could not touch any part of the aircraft without wearing gloves. There would have been no problem in frying eggs on the wings. Incidentally, even in the Far East heat we always flew wearing gloves and leather gauntlets in case of fire in the cockpit.

However, every day we would see big clouds rising up over New Guinea and coming towards us, and when they reached us, regularly as clockwork, at two o'clock we would have a tropical downpour. When not flying we would lounge on the luke-warm sea in a hole blasted out of the coral by the Americans, while small native boys would 'shin' up the surrounding trees and cut down and open coconuts for us.

While at Ponam we were joined by a replacement pilot, Colin Campbell, an old Lorettonian with whom I had been at school, so we had quite a party. Colin became my number two.

However, this was not to last and we landed back on *Ruler* on 28 June.

Truk, 14 and 15 June (Operation Inmate)

Truk is an island north-east of Manus and about half way to Guam. While we were at Ponam, the task force to hit Truk included *Ruler* as a spare 'deck', which worked out well, as six Seafires which had lost touch with their carrier *Implacable*, due to poor weather conditions, landed with us. The last one hit the round down (the stern end of the flight deck which curves downward) and slid up the deck, breaking up as it did so, the pilot stepping out unhurt. Our air sea rescue Walrus aircraft had been ranged aft, ready to take off if required, so when the Seafires arrived it had to be pushed forward of the barrier in a hurry. With all the activity it had not been secured and just as the last Seafire landed the ship ran into a squall and the Walrus rose, ever so gently off the deck, fell away to port, crashed into the sea and sank.

On 27 June *Ruler* collected me from Ponam and then returned to Manus on 3 July. Leaving there on 5 July, we were again engaged in combat air patrols. On one CAP I was flying as No 2 to Lt (A) Dennis Papworth when we were ordered to do a 'square search' for an unidentified ship on the radar screen. The No 2's aircraft always uses more fuel because of the weaving to protect his leader's tail. At the limit of our search we were some 230 nautical miles from *Ruler* and, on reporting 'fuel minus' (ie petrol gauges showing less than half tanks of fuel), we were recalled by the aircraft direction officer (ADO). The ADO gave a reliable reciprocal course to steer, and good navigation and flying ensured we made contact with *Ruler* without having to search for her. The maintenance crew who refuelled my aircraft calculated I had less than ten gallons left in the tanks – another near shave!

Ruler's Hellcats again flew CAP over the fleet train while they were refuelling and replenishing the fleet on 13 July. When not engaged in CAPs we spent a lot of time exercising the fleet train with dummy kamikaze attacks. On 21 July I had to collect a Hellcat from another escort carrier, *Arbiter*. This entailed my being transferred by breeches buoy from *Ruler* to the destroyer *Quality*, then to the destroyer *Undine*, and finally to *Arbiter*.

On another occasion I was transferred to the destroyer *Dauntless* and then on to the escort carrier *Chaser*, again to collect a Hellcat and fly it back to *Ruler*. Once when *Ruler*'s deck was unavailable I had to land on another escort carrier, *Speaker*, at the end of my CAP and later the same day I took off from *Speaker* to take part in my second CAP, having been refuelled there.

While carrying out dummy kamikaze attacks on the fleet train on 2 August, Lt (A) Vercoe slid over the port side on take-off due to a very heavy swell.

On 6 and 9 August nuclear bombs were dropped by the USAAF on Hiroshima and Nagasaki. From the beginning of August we were mostly employed doing fighter direction and dummy kamikaze exercises with various carriers and cruisers up until 15 August when Japan capitulated.

Although Japan had capitulated and we 'spliced the main brace' to celebrate VJ Day, the following day several kamikazes attacked the task force again, so we were all back to action stations. This prompted the following signal to all ships from 'C in C': "All enemy aircraft approaching the fleet are now to be shot down in a friendly manner." When this was sorted out we had a well deserved second VJ Day and 'spliced the main brace' again.

On 18 August HMS *Duke of York*, a large RN battleship, joined us, cruising around somewhere off Japan until 28 August when we steamed north towards Tokyo. We entered Tokyo Bay the next day

My last flight was on 23 August and brought my total flying hours to 843, with 59 successful deck landings. I understand I was the only *Ruler* pilot not to have had a 'prang' deck landing. Unfortunately, there was no bonus from their Lordships! In fact, the squadron pilots and maintenance crews did not even get a thank-you for all their efforts.

When we saw Japan we had spent 57 days at sea, the longest time a Royal Navy ship had been at sea out of sight of land since Nelson's day.

On 31 August *Ruler* entered Tokyo Bay. The port side of the flight deck was lined with aircraft with port wings and the starboard side with aircraft with starboard wings, and ranged on the 'round down' (right at the stern) was my aircraft 'Moonshiner', the only fully serviceable aircraft left on board.

This would be an appropriate time to explain that I had christened my aircraft 'Moonshiner' and had had the name painted on the engine cowling. The reason was that I rather liked the song 'Moonshiner.' As I have said earlier, I was always a non-singer at school, but at a certain stage of an evening, with convivial company,

An Avenger being catapulted from HMS Ruler.

Hellcat landing.

Boyd and his Hellcat 'Moonshiner'.

The US Third Fleet and British Pacific Fleet at anchor in Tokyo Bay, viewed from HMS Indefatigable.

I was known to join in the singing, albeit out of tune; but I knew the words!

I'm a rambler, I'm a gambler, I'm a long way from home,
And if you don't like me just leave me alone.
I'll eat when I'm hungry, I'll drink when I'm dry,
If the moonshine don't kill me, I'll live till I die. [etc]

On 2 September the Japanese surrender was signed aboard USS *Missouri*. This was a most impressive day in Tokyo Bay as from early morning a succession of huge US aircraft circled Mount Fujiyama and Tokyo Bay before landing. There must have been many thousands of aircraft as a show of US strength.

Missouri was moored a short distance from *Ruler* and we were able to watch the whole ceremony. Captains of many of the British and American ships were invited to attend. From the flight deck of *Ruler* we had a great view of the proceedings and saw people like Tojo, the head of the Japanese government, in his top hat and black tails, General MacArthur, the US Army commander, in a sparkling uniform covered in 'gongs' (medals) and dozens of white-uniformed naval captains. It was a marvellous sight in the brilliant sunshine.

While we were in Tokyo we sadly learned that the officer, Jack Habberfield, a New Zealander, who had escorted Frank Hollywood's body home to Bangor for burial, was later shot down in the Pacific operations. During a bombing run against the Japanese mainland island of Honshu, he had been captured and beheaded by sword in front of all the other POWs at the camp to which he was taken. We learnt later that the Japanese officer who was responsible for this atrocity was eventually traced, tried and executed.

On 5 September 885 Squadron pilots were transferred to *Indefatigable* for transport to Sydney, to provide space for released POWs aboard *Ruler*.

Throughout the squadron story there was a dramatic change of personnel. There were, for example, five successive and experienced Senior Pilots: Lts Moore, Lang, Papworth, Brooshooft and myself (the senior pilot of a squadron was the next in command of the squadron after the CO). One of three COs, Lt Cmdr 'Tiny' Devonald, won the RAF's DFC over Normandy in recognition of 885 Squadron's efforts in the invasion of Normandy.

Back in Sydney we were billeted in a transit camp situated under the grandstand of Warwick Farm Racecourse. While there I had a phone call from my brother, a submariner, whom I had not seen for several years. He had arrived in Sydney in a submarine to supply power to the Sydney General Hospital as there was an electricity strike on in Sydney. I gave him directions to get to Warwick Farm and we had quite a party.

After a brief stay at Warwick Farm, I joined the troopship *Dominion Monarch* in early November, in charge of the squadron personnel, to return to UK. Conditions were very cramped on board and a group of RAF pilots refused to sail in those conditions and walked off the ship. However, I was only too happy to be on my way home

After a six-week voyage, with stops at Colombo and Port Said, we arrived at Southampton shortly before Christmas. On arrival I had to write out over 200 travel warrants for my squad and send them on leave. I had a few books of warrants left over, which I used, over the next six months indefinite leave, for trips between Belfast and London.

I was finally demobilised in April 1946.

Chapter 10
Thoughts

At the start of the war the Royal Navy was so out of date it was unbelievable. The hierarchy thought big ships, ie battleships, were 'the thing' and had no interest in the flying side of the Navy. In a two-seater aircraft the observer was the captain of the ship, if senior, not the pilot, which was absolutely ridiculous considering the type of aircraft we were using at the time. Most of the ships during the war were mainly manned by RNVR officers and men. This was even more evident in the Royal Naval Air Squadrons.

This brings to mind a couple of uncomplimentary sayings. The RN types were known to us as our 'paid hands' – the fellows who looked after our ships for us in peacetime. The second concerns sailing: "The three most useless things to bring aboard a sailing yacht are an umbrella, a wheelbarrow and a naval officer."

When we arrived at HMS Daedalus, Lee-on-Solent, the headquarters of the Fleet Air Arm, as an operational squadron, they even still had a 'gun room' for junior officers and a 'wardroom' for senior officers. On our first night there as an operational squadron, we sorted that problem out by charging the dividing wall with ornamental lances taken from the wall. The following day the dividing wall was removed.

The next thing that the old 'codgers' wanted was that we should change into uniform before coming into the 'wardroom' for lunch, even though we had just returned from a 'bombardment spotting' sortie over Normandy and were due to go back again in an hour and might not get back. They didn't seem to know that there was a war going on! They just sat there with their pink gins and complained about we young chaps – who were fighting the war for them!

I was most embarrassed by the facilities supplied by the old 'dead beat' officers at Lee-on-Solent (HMS Daedalus) when the RAF and USN squadrons arrived at Lee. When they saw the squalor and discomfort of the pilots' ready rooms, they hit the roof and next day all our pilot ready rooms were equipped with comfortable armchairs, tables, carpets and all the latest papers and magazines, as well as coffee machines and a supply of sandwiches.

To those of us not steeped in naval tradition, their lordships' obsession with big guns and battleships seemed pigheaded and blinkered. It seems hard to believe now, but many admirals and senior officers until the end of 1941 believed that you could actually defend ships and fleets against enemy aircraft with anti-aircraft guns. This myth was finally and painfully put to rest when the *Prince of Wales* and *Repulse* were sunk by Japanese aircraft off eastern Malaya on 10 December 1941, just three days after Pearl Harbor was attacked. Many people consider it was a criminal decision to send the ships, the pride of the Royal Navy, to sea without any air support.

Also in 1941 the Italian fleet had been attacked at night in Taranto harbour and virtually destroyed by Swordfish aircraft from one of our aircraft carriers in the Mediterranean. However, this was hardly mentioned by the Admiralty as it did not support their 'big guns' mentality.

About this time the German battle cruisers *Scharnhorst* and *Gneisenau*, and the cruiser *Prince Eugen* had escaped from Brest and had run up the Channel in broad daylight without our ships or the RAF being able to do anything to stop them. 825 Squadron's attack with six Swordfish, led by Eugene Edmond, failed because these German ships had proper air cover in the shape of 40 Me 109s which shot down the six Swordfish, un-intercepted by the ten RAF Spitfires which eventually turned up too late to protect them. The Admiralty put out the story that the Swordfish met a curtain of anti-aircraft fire which shot them all down; again this suited their 'big guns' mentality!

It is sad to think that when our Seafires at Ballyhalbert were grounded in 1944 because they were not suitable for dive bombing missions (due to the weakness of their folding wings under dive bombing stresses), the message was not passed on to the powers that be. As a result, nearly a year later a number of Seafires working with the British Pacific Fleet lost their wings when pulling out of dive bombing runs, killing the pilots.

All our American-built aircraft were ditched over the side off Australia once the war was over under the terms of 'lend–lease.' What an awful waste!

Chapter 11
Post-War

While waiting to be demobbed I was working in the London Stock Exchange as a 'blue button' (a very junior clerk on the dealing floor) and used to meet up with several other ex–Fleet Air Arm types like myself at the RNVR Club or the Brevet Club most evenings. I managed to live reasonably well there, being paid by the Navy with flying pay, by ADM & Co of Belfast and L & Co of London.

When I had nearly finished my tour in London and due to go back to Belfast, I thought of joining Aer Lingus who were paying pilots £1,000 per annum, while I would be starting at only £200 per annum in Belfast. I rang my father one night to tell him my thoughts. After a long conversation I decided not to go to Oxford for a twin engine conversion course the next day to become an Aer Lingus pilot, but instead to return to Belfast and stockbroking.

My ex-squadron colleague, Bill Wallace, with whom I was to have joined Aer Lingus, went up to Oxford and joined. He ended up a senior pilot with Aer Lingus. I used to meet him for many years at Fleet Air Arm reunions on HMS *Caroline* in Belfast harbour.

Back home in Ulster in March 1947 I went to Londonderry Air Charter at Newtownards airfield to hire an aircraft. I showed my log book and did a couple of 'circuits and bumps' with the resident instructor in a de Havilland Hornet Moth, which was a bit like a closed-in Tiger Moth. When he was satisfied that I could fly he got out and I took off again for an hour's 'local flying'. That meant that I was to remain in sight of the airfield. However, local flying was not my intention at all. I set out for Monaghan town to beat up a friend's house and to beat up my fiancee's house outside Clones, both in the Republic of Ireland. We had had the largest snowfall for years, so the whole country was covered. I had no map and had not plotted a proper course before taking off, as I reckoned I knew Northern

Ireland pretty well. However, I had not reckoned with the whole country being totally covered in snow. So it was not surprising that very soon after take-off I realised that I was lost. When I saw a town with a signpost on the outskirts, I flew down low to read it and found the road to Armagh and Middletown which I then followed. Approaching the border crossing, I flew a mile or so over to the left so that the customs men could not read my number. I beat up my friend's house in Monaghan and then, realising that I had used up half of my fuel, I had to turn for home. Again I got lost, but then found Dungannon, from where I made it back to Newtownards. All very careless and not conducive to a long life! That was the end of my flying career!

Since 1947 we have had an annual *Ruler*/885 Squadron reunion in London. At first there were 30 to 40 attending, with the ship's officers outnumbering the squadron officers, but in later years, with only about ten attending, there were more squadron than ship's officers. When we had joined up we had all been in our teens or early twenties. The ship's officers were much older. To us, anyone more than twenty-five was nearly 'over the hill!' Finally, full marks to John Robson, who organised these, the only known ship/squadron reunions.

Long Post-War

During the Gulf War it was interesting to see that the USS *Missouri* was bombarding the Iraqi troops and positions in Kuwait with her 16-inch guns, just as she had bombarded the German troops and positions in Normandy during that invasion, as well as receiving the Japanese surrender in 1945.

Appendix I
Record of Service

Unit		Dates
24 EFTS	Sealand, Cheshire	22 April–17 June '42
31 SFTS	Kingston, Ontario, Canada	15 July–6 Nov '42
9 AFU	Errol, Scotland	4–23 Jan '43
RNAS	Yeovilton, Somerset	22 Feb–28 May '43
HMS Argus	Firth of Clyde, Scotland	17–22 May '43
NAFU	Warmwell, Somerset	23–29 May '43
RNAS	Worthy Dorn, Hants	19 June–7 Oct '43
RNAS	Hinstock, Shrops	6–12 Sept '43
RNAS	St Merryn, Cornwall	7–13 Oct '43
10 NOTU	Chivenor, Devon	13 Oct–6 Dec '43
RNAS	Machrihanish, Scotland	21 Jan–14 Feb '44
RNAS	Lee-on-Solent, Hants	15–21 Feb '44
RNAS	St Merryn, Cornwall	21 Feb–2 Apr '44
RNAS	Henstridge, Somerset	2–22 Apr '44
RAF	Dundonald, Ayrshire	22 Apr–6 May '44
RAF	Heathfield, Ayrshire	6–13 May '44
RNAS	Lee-on-Solent, Hants	13 May–20 July '44
RAF	Ballyhalbert, Co Down	1 Aug–15 Dec '44
HMS *Ruler*		15 Dec '44–5 Sept '45
HMS *Indefatigable*	5–12 Sept '45	
Transit Camp	Warwick Farm Racecourse	12 Sept–1 Nov '45
Dominion Monarch (troopship)		1 Nov–22 Dec '45

Appendix II
Airfields, Airstrips and Aircraft Carriers Landed on

Sealand	Cheshire	England
Wolverhampton		England
Kingston	Ontario	Canada
Gananoque	Ontario	Canada
Picton	Ontario	Canada
Errol	Perthshire	Scotland
Yeovilton	Somerset	England
Zeals		England
Warmwell	Somerset	England
Worthy Down	Hants	England
Gosport	Hants	England
Hinstock	Shropshire	England
Triligga	Cornwall	England
Chivenor	Devon	England
St Merryn	Cornwall	England
St Eval	Cornwall	England
Machrihanish	Mull of Kintyre	Scotland
Burscough	Lancs	England
Lee-on-Solent	Hants	England
Fearne		Scotland
Skebrae	Orkney Isles	Scotland
Hatston	Orkney Isles	Scotland
Donniebristle	Fifeshire	Scotland

Haverford West		Wales
Henstridge	Somerset	England
Stretton		England
Dundonald	Ayrshire	Scotland
Heathfield	Ayrshire	Scotland
Thorny Island		England
Ballyhalbert	Co Down	N Ireland
Sydenham	Belfast	N Ireland
Eglinton	Londonderry	N Ireland
Langford Lodge	Antrim	N Ireland
Burton Wood		England
Prestwick	Renfrewshire	Scotland
Renfrew	Renfrewshire	Scotland
Schofields	New South Wales	Australia
Jervis Bay	New South Wales	Australia
Mascot	Sydney NSW	Australia
Ponam	Admiralty Islands	Papua New Guinea
Momote	Admiralty Islands	Papua New Guinea
Lae		Papua New Guinea
Milne Bay		Papua New Guinea
Townsville	North Queensland	Australia
Archer Field	Brisbane	Australia

HMS Argus
HMS Ruler
HMS Victorious
HMS Chaser
HMS Speaker
HMS Arbiter

Appendix III
Aircraft Flown

Aircraft	Engine
Tiger Moth	Gypsy Moth
Harvard II	Wasp S3HI
Master I	Kestrel
Master II	Mercury
Hurricane I	Merlin III
Fulmar II	Merlin XXXII
Hurricane IIB	Merlin XX
Procter I & II	Gypsy Queen II
Swordfish	Pegasus III
Lysander III	Mercury XX
Oxford	Cheetahs (2)
Seafire IB	Merlin XLV
Martinet I	Mercury XXX
Seafire III	Merlin LV
Seafire LIII	Merlin LV M
Spitfire IB	Merlin XLV
Spitfire VB	Merlin XLV
Seafire IIC	Merlin XXXII
Hellcat	Pratt & Whitney Double Wasp
Reliant	Pratt & Whitney Wasp

Appendix IV
Particulars of 885 Squadron and HMS *Ruler*

885 Squadron's air power

With initial Pacific complement: 18 Hellcats and 4 Avengers

Missiles: air-to-surface, (anti-submarine), 5 inch: eight per Hellcat, eight per Avenger.

Bombs: 1,000 lb: two per Hellcat, two per Avenger (2,000 lb per aircraft)

Depth charges: four per Avenger

Maximum squadron bombing capacity: 44,000 lb (20 tons)

Fixed wing guns: 50 cal (0.5in) Browning: six per Hellcat, two per Avenger

HMS Ruler

Hull type: US Maritime Commission C3 – S1 – A3

Class: USN 'Prince William', RN 'Ruler'

Pennant Nos: USN (CVE)50, RN D72, BPF A731

Displacement tonnage: 15,012 tons (fully loaded)

Length overall: 495 feet

Length of flight deck: 80 feet (tapered)

Beam at waterline: 69.5 feet; at flight deck – 108.5 feet; over sponsons – 88 feet

Draft at full load: 25.5 feet

HMS Ruler's Power Train

Two Foster Wheeler D-type boilers

Working pressure: 525 pounds per square inch

Allis Chalmers turbine: 8500 shaft hp geared to propeller

Consumption: three tons per hour at 18 knots

Duration, without supplying other ships: about 45 days at 18 knots

Aviation fuel bunker capacity: 166,625 gallons (643 tons)

HMS Ruler's Aircraft Carrying Capacity

While ferrying: 80 fighter aircraft (reported as maximum carried by an RN CVE)

While flying: 24 Hellcats; or 18 Hellcats and four Avengers; or 15 Hellcats, six Corsairs and three Avengers

HMS Ruler's Armament

Two stern-mounted 5 inch guns

Eight twin-mounted 40mm Bofors guns

14 twin-mounted 20mm Oerlikon guns

Seven single 20mm Oerlikon guns

Total long and short range gunnery armament: 53

Ship's company: including officers, and without squadron – about 550

Squadron aircrew: 30 pilots, five observers and five Tel/Air gunners – about 40

Squadron surface teams: including technical, stores and administration – about 120

Total ship's complement, including squadron – about 710

Much of this data was complied by the Navigator John Robson, with assistance from Andrew Auld (engineroom), Ben Bolt (Air Dept), Dennis Papworth (Squadron) and Bob Vardy (Gunnery Dept).

Appendix V
Chronology of HMS *Ruler*

1943

Aug 21 Ships launched at Tacoma, named *St Joseph*

Dec 22 USS *St Joseph* handed over to RN by USN; commissioned as HMS *Ruler*

      23 Arrived Vancouver BC for Admiralty modifications

1944

Feb 15 885 Squadron re-formed with Seafires for Overlord, the invasion of Europe

Feb 25 Ship's company joined

Mar 20 Sailed Esquimalt BC for Norfolk VA

Apr 21 Sailed Norfolk after loading aircraft

      24 Sailed New York on first aircraft ferrying passage in convoy

May 30 Sailed New York on second aircraft ferrying passage in convoy

Jun 6 D-Day; 885 Squadron in action over Normandy

      24 Arrived Newport, S Wales, for conversion to assault carrier

Aug   885 Squadron assigned to *Ruler*. Re-equipped with Hellcats at Ballyhalbert, NI

Sep 17 Sailed Newport, S Wales, conversion completed

      30 Sailed Greenock for third aircraft ferrying passage

Oct 4 Main turbine damaged. Proceeded independently to Norfolk VA

Nov 7 Sailed New York, third aircraft ferrying passage in convoy

Dec 15 885 Squadron joined *Ruler* in Belfast for working up in Firth of Clyde

1945

Jan 28 Sailed Greenock for Sydney to join British Pacific Fleet

Feb 9 Arrived Alexandria for repair of storm-damaged flight deck

Mar 16 Arrived Sydney. 885 Squadron later flown ashore

Apr 15 Sailed Sydney for Leyte, Philippines

25 Arrived Leyte Gulf, joined British Pacific Fleet, Task Force 57 of USN 5th Fleet

May 3 Sailed Leyte Gulf for replenishment area Cootie, Operation Iceberg II

6 First of five replenishments for TF 57 in Iceberg II; 885 Squadron provided air cover (CAP), anti-submarine patrols (ASP) and searches, flying from *Ruler*

31 Arrived Manus, Admiralty Islands

Jun 12–17 Operation Inmate, *Ruler* acted as spare deck during raid on Truk

July 5 Sailed Manus for operations off Japan

13 First of seven replenishments for TF 57 in operations off Japan; 885 Squadron provided CAP, ASP and other tasks, flying from *Ruler*

Aug 15 BPF ceased offensive operations

28 Final flying operations by 885 Squadron and *Ruler*

31 Anchored in Tokyo Bay

Sep 5 885 Squadron personnel transferred to HMS *Indefatigable*

15 Sailed Tokyo Bay with 445 released POWs and internees

27 Arrived Sydney

Oct 21 885 Squadron disbanded in Sydney
24 Sailed Sydney for UK
Dec 3 Arrived Glasgow. Prepared for return of ship to USN
1946
Jan 8 Sailed Southampton for Norfolk VA
19 Arrived Norfolk VA
29 Ship de-commissioned and handed back to USN

This chronology was compiled by the Navigator John Robson assisted by Ben Bolt (Air Dept). The dates were mostly taken from *Ruler*'s fair copy deck logs which run from the end of February 1944 until the end of December 1945, and from 885 Squadron's log books. Dates outside this period were obtained from various sources, some of which are uncertain.

Appendix VI
Badges, Mottoes and Battle Honours

The heraldic description of HMS *Ruler*'s badge is:

Field:
  Azure
Badge:
  A dexter gauntlet proper grasping a baton ensigned to the dexter with a crown and held fessewise gold.
Ship's Motto:
  "Through vigilance"
Battle honours:
  Atlantic 1944
  Okinawa 1945

The heraldic description of 885 Squadron's badge is:

Field:
  Azure issuant from water barry engrailed white and azure flames proper therein a cat affronte black.
Squadron's Motto:
  "Celerime"
Battle honours:
  Malta Convoys 1941–42
  North Africa 1942–43
  Sicily 1943
  Normandy 1944
  Okinawa 1945

115

Appendix VII
Plan of HMS *Ruler's* flight deck

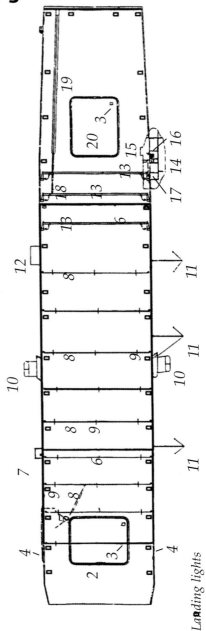

116

Bridge Island

1 Bridge
2 Air defence position
3 Combat information centre
4 Wheelhouse
5 Charthouse
6 Searchlight platform
7 Captain's sea cabin
8 Navigator's sea cabin
9 Gyro compass repeater
10 Flight control position
11 Urinal

Flight Deck

1 Rounddown
2 Aft aircraft lift
3 Lift control position
4 Aircraft derrick stowed
5 Aircraft derrick, alternative position
6 Expansion joint
7 Deck landing control position
8 Aircraft arrester wire
9 Yielding arrester wire yoke
10 Funnel
11 Aircraft stowage outrigger
12 Aircraft ditching ramp
13 Aircraft safety barrier
14 Bridge island
15 Aircraft control position
16 Captain's sea cabin
17 Navigator's sea cabin
18 Aircraft-launching cleat
19 Aircraft-catapult track
20 Forward aircraft lift

Bibliography

Crossley, Commander R 'Mike' , *They Gave Me A Seafire* , Parapress Ltd, 1994 (2nd ed)

'Round Down' (Goadsby, Dick), *Wings of the Wind*, Auribus Publications, 1987

Smith, Peter C, *Task Force 57*

Some Members of Her Ship's Company and Squadron Personnel (Robson, John and Bolt, Ben), *Ruler's Reign: The Story of a Lend Lease Escort Carrier and Her Squadron 1943–1946*, HMS Ruler and 885 Squadron Association, 2000

The Fleet Air Arm Song Book , np, nd

Index

Italics indicate an illustration of the subject matter.

24 EFTS (Elementary Flying Training School) 16

31 SFTS (Service Flying Training School) 22–3

748 Squadron 39, *41*

755 Squadron 36

756 Squadron 36

759 Squadron 31

772 Squadron 40

808 Squadron 48

825 Squadron 102

885 Squadron 40, 42, 44, 49, 51, 57–8, *59*, 61, 65, 69, 72–3, 77, 83, *85*, 93, 99–100, 105

886 Squadron 48, 58

897 Squadron 48

1772 Squadron 70, 83

Aase Maersk 89
Activity, HMS 72
Adelphi Cinema, Bangor 6
Admiralty 73, 102
Admiralty Islands 84, *92*, 93
Aer Lingus 104
Air Training Corps (ATC) 11, 39
Alexandria 72
Americas' Cup 7
Anson 53

Arbiter, HMS 93, 95
Archer Field 93
Ardmillan 57
Argus, HMS 36
Armagh (city) 105
Arndale 89
Arran 47
Atlantic Ocean 13, 20, 29, 60
Auster 61
Australia 72, *74*, 76–7, 80, 82–3, 103
Avenger 70, 72, 93, 97
Avon 86
Ayr, RAF 47
— RNAS 67
Ayrshire 47

Bal-Carat 89
Ballyhalbert airfield 58, *59*, 60–1, 63–4, 102
Ballymena 23
Bangalore 12
Bangor 6–7, *8*, 13, 20, 25, 37, 99
— Golf Club 62
Barnstable 40
Bantham, G *85*
Bassett, Sub-Lt Bertie 40, 50, *50*, 55, 57
Bayeux 54
Bay of Biscay 72
Bazenville 53

119

BBC 11
Belfast 6, 13, 20, 29, 43, 55–6, 58, 61, 64, 70, 73, 100, 104
Bentley 9
Bira of Siam, Prince 9, 39, 41
Bitter Lakes 73
Black Prince, HMS 89
Bondi Beach 80
Borneo 84
Bowles, Lt J 85, 89, *91*
Boyd, Austin 13, 29, 57
Boyne, Battle of the 29
Brest 102
Brevet Club 104
Brisbane 93
Britannia 7
British Pacific Fleet 83, *98*, 103
Brooshooft, Lt M 85, 99
'B' Specials, Royal Ulster Constabulary 11
Bugatti 9
Burscough 42, 48
Bute, Isle of 69

Cadbury, Peter 14
Caen 50, 53–6
Caledonian Canal 44
Calgary 56
Campbell, Colin 94
Canada 20, *21*, 22–5, *27*, 29–30, 80
Caproni's ballroom 25
Caroline, HMS 104
Cary, Dave 56
Carrickiola 9

Cedardale 86
Ceylon 73
Chamberlain, Neville 9
Chamen, Sub-Lt B 85
Chaser, HMS 93, 95
Cherbourg 53
— peninsula 53, 56
Chesil Beach 36
Chester 16, 18, *19*, 56, 63
Churchill, WS 73
Clendinning, Harry 14, 22, 23, 25, 31
Clones 104
Clyde, Firth of 29, 36, 40, 47, 67, 80
Cobham, Alan 6
Colombo 73, 76, 100
Comber 12, 51
Condor 13
Connecticut 28
Coral Sea 34
Cornwall 39, 42
Corsair 70, 72, 90
Coulthurst, Sub-Lt K 85
Crane 86, 89
Crawford, George 23–4, *23*
Cultra 14

Dad's Army 11
Daedalus, HMS 14, 42, 48–9, 56, 101
Dakota (aircraft) 53–4, 93
Dauntless, HMS 95
D-Day 49–51
Dee, River 19

Devonald, CO 'Tiny' 42, 42, 61, 100
DH 86 44, 47
Dingledale 89
Dixon, Freddie 9
Dominion Monarch 100
Don, Kay 9
Down, Co 6, 51–2, *59*, *62*
Dowsett, Sub-Lt Les 70, *85*, *88*, 89
Drem airfield 10
Duke of York, HMS 96
Dundonald (Scotland) 47
Dungannon 105

Edinburgh 10–13
Edmond, Eugene 102
Edwards, Jimmy 23
Eglinton airfield 61
English Channel 50, 102
Enterprise, HMS 47
Erebus, HMS 53
Errol airfield 31
Esk, River 10

Fairey Fulmar *32*, 33, 36
Far East 56, 60, 80, 94
Faruk, King 73
Fearne airfield 44
Fencer, HMS *78*
Firefly 70, 83
Fisher, Sub-Lt Jim 67
Fleet Air Arm 13, 30, *35*, 36, 66, 69, 101, 104
Flying Fortress 60
Focke-Wulf 190 51

Formidable, HMS 86
Forth, Firth of 10
Forth Bridge 10
France 56
Furnival, Sub-Lt Mike 67, *85*

Gallaher's factory 72
Galle Face Hotel 73
Gananoque 27
Gananoque airfield 25, *27*
George V, King 7
German East Africa 64
Germany 9
Gibraltar 72
Gillespie, General Rollo 51
Glasgow 10, 40
Gloster Gladiator 31, *32*
Gneisenau *102*
Goadsby, Sub-Lt Dick 67, *85*
Goebbels, Joseph 89
Gone With The Wind 37
Gosport 14, 16
Gosport, RNAS 37
Gransha Point 60–1
Greyabbey court 61
Groomsport 6
Guam 94
Gulf War 105
Gwebarra 9
Gypsy Major 16

Habberfield, Jack 99
Halifax (Nova Scotia) 20

121

Hall, Freddie 9
Hallett, Commander 'Buster' 56
Handley, Lt T *85*
Hardwick, Sub-Lt 80
Harlow, Jean 6
Hartland, Sub-Lt D *85*
Hartford (Connecticut) 28
Harvard II 22, 25, *27*
Hates, Sub-Lt R *85*
Hatston 44
Haverford West 44
Hawarden 61, 63
Headline Shipping Co 29
Heathfield, RAF 48
Heavenly Body 72
Hellcat II 63, *65*, 66–7, 70, 72–3, 77, 80–1, *82*, 83–4, 89–90, *91*, 93, 95, 97–8
Hell's Angels 6
Henstridge, RNAS 74
Heron, HMS 31
Heyden Stone 29
Hinstock, RNAS 39
Hiroshima 95
Hitler, Adolf 89
Hollywood, Frank 13–14, *19*, 23, 31, *31*, 99
Home Guard (see also Local Defence Force) 11–12, 29
Honshu 99
Horne, Sub-Lt (A) George 67, *85*
Hornet Moth 104
Howe, Earl 9
Howe, HMS 86

Hurricane 13, 31, 33, 36

Ilchester 33
Imperial Services Club (Sydney) 80
Implacable, HMS 94
Indefatigable, HMS 86, *98*, 99
Indomitable, HMS 84, 86, 89
Indian Army 12
Indian Ocean 73, *85*
International Bridge (Canada) 22, 24–5, *27*
Inverness 44
Ireland 29, 60
Irish Free State 14, 60
Iron Bridge 19, *19*
Isle of Man 39

Japan 96, 99
Japanese government 99
Japanese navy 89
Jervis Bay 80–1, 83

kamikaze attacks 89, 93, 95–6
Kelly, Joe 11
Kennett, Sub-Lt (A) 57
Kestrel, HMS 36
Kilkeel 7
Killinchy 11–12, 29, 57
Killinchy LDF 11
Killinchy Orange hall 12
Killyleagh 11
Kingfisher 48
King George V, HMS 86

Kingston (Ontario) 21, 22–5, 29
Kircubbin 58, 59, 60, 64
Kirkiston airfield 60–1
Knowe Head 12
Kuwait 105

L & Co 104
Lae 093
Lake Ontario 22, 24
Lamarr, Hedy 72
Lamlash 40, 69
Lamour, Dorothy 28
Lancashire 42
Landrail, HMS 40
Lang, Lt (A) Sam 67, 85, 99
Larne 13
Lea Francis 9
Lee-on-Solent 14, 40, 42, 49–51, 53–7, 101
Letitia 20, 20, 22
Lewis, Sub-Lt D 85
Leyte 84, 86
Leyte Bay 84
Lightning 51
Local Defence Force (LDF – see also Home Guard) 11
London 13, 37, 40, 100, 104–5
London Stock Exchange 104
Londonderry 61
Londonderry, Lord 9
Londonderry Air Charter 104
Loretto School 10–11
Lysander 23, 36, 38

MacIlwaine, Douglas 37
MacArthur, General Douglas 99
Machrihanish, RNAS 40
Mackworth, Group Captain 22
Madden, 'Titch' 55
Malaya 102
Manly Beach 80
Manus 84, 92, 93–5
Martinet 36, 40
Mascot airport 77
Master 31, 36
Mediterranean Sea 102
Messerschmitt 109 50–1, 53, 102
Metcalfe, Lt (A) 57
Middletown 105
Milne Bay 93
Missouri, USS 99, 105
Moncton 20, 22
Moncur, CPO 70
Monaghan (town) 104–5
Monaghan Bank 60
Monote 93
Montreal 20
Moore, Lt 99
Mount Fujiyama 99
Mount Livinia 73
Mount Stewart 9
Mourne Grange School 7, 10
Murrayfield 11
Musselburgh 10

Nabthorpe, HMS 77
Nagasaki 95

Napier, HMS 86
Napier, Sub-Lt (A) Horace 70, *85*, 90
Neill, Arthur 37
Nelson, HMS 9, 50
Nepal 86, 89
Nevada, USS 52–3
New Brunswick 20
Newfield 10
Newfoundland, HMS 73
New Guinea see Papua New Guinea
Newtownards 7, *62*, 105
Newtownards airfield 104
New York City 28–9
New York (state) 24
New Zealand 14, 37, 99
Norfolk (Virginia) 37
Norman, HMS 86, 89
Normandy 50, 63, 100–1, 105
Normandy 28
Norman Rodgers airfield *21*, 22
Northern Ireland 6, 14, 58, 60, 104
North Queensland 93
Nuvolari 9

O'Dea, Jimmy 9
Officer Training Corps (OTC) 11
Old Bushmills Distillery 13, 57
'Old Man of Hoy' 44
Olivier, Laurence 14
Orne, River 55
Ontario *21*, 22–3, *27*, 31
Operation Iceberg II 86, *91*

Operation Inmate 94
Operation Overlord 50, 55, 57
Orkney Islands 43
Orlock 20
Orr, Sub-Lt Peter 70, 93
Ouistraham golf club 50, 54
Oxford 104
'Oxford' aircraft 39

Pacific Ocean 72–3, 86, *87–8*, 89, 99
Papua New Guinea 83–4, 93–4
Papworth, Lt (A) Dennis *85*, 95, 99
Parker, Jeff 22
Parnell, Reg 9
Pastroudi's 73
Pearl Harbor 102
Perth 31
Perthshire 31
Pheasant 86, 89
Philippine Islands 84
Pickie Pool 6
Pompey (see also Portsmouth) 16, 37
Ponam Island *92*, 94
Port Said 73, 100
Portsmouth (see also Pompey) 13, 16, 37, 40, 49
Prince Edward Bay 24
Prince Eugen 102
Prince of Wales, HMS 102
Proctor II 36, *38*
Pyrmount No 12 dock 77, *78*

Quality, HMS 95

Quebec 29
Queen Elizabeth 29
Queenborough, HMS 98
Quettehou 52
Quilliam, HMS 89
Quincey, USS 54

Ramilles, HMS 50
Reading 55
Red Sea 73
Republic of Ireland 104
Repulse, HMS 102
Ribbentrop, Count Joachim von 9
Richardson, Ralph 14
Riley 9
Robson, Lt John 64, 72, 105
Roc 40
Rodney, HMS 9
Rollins, Sub-Lt 50
Romano's 80
Roosevelt, Franklin D 73
Rosyth 10
Rothesay Bay 69
Routley, Lt-Cmdr J *85*
Royal Air Force (RAF) 12, 16, 33, 53, 102
Royal Air Force Northern Ireland (RAFNI) 60
Royal Naval Volunteer Reserve (RNVR) 14, 67, 101
RNVR Club 104
Royal Navy (RN) 12–13, 61, 101–2
Royal North of Ireland Yacht Club (Cultra) 14

Royal Troon golf club 47
Royal Ulster Yacht Club, Bangor 7
Ruler, HMS64, 66–7, *68*, 69, 71, 72–3, *74*, *76*, 76–7, *78*, 80, 83–4, *85*, 86, *88*, 89–90, *91*, 93–6, *97*, 99, 105

St Anne's Cathedral 64
St Eval 39
St Lawrence River 22, 25, *26*
St Merryn, RNAS 39–40, 42–4, 47
St Vincent, HMS 14–16
Sakishima Gunto 86
San Adolpho 86
San Amado 89
San Ambrosia 86
Sardinia 72
Scharnhorst 102
Schneider Trophy 22
Schofields airfield 77, *79*, 80
Scotland 9–10, 36, 44, 47
Scrabo Tower *62*
Seafire III 39, *41*, 42–3, *45*–6, 47–9, 51, 54, 56, *59*, 60, 63, 70, 81, 94, 102–3
Sea Hurricane *32*, 33
Sealand 16, 18
Shamrock V 7
Sherry, Pat 14
Short Brothers 16
Simpson, Lt Harry 64, *85*
Skebrae 43–4
Skua 40
Smiles, Chris 28

125

Smiles, Sir Walter 28
Snipe Sailing Club, Whiterock 9
Solway Firth 44
Somerset 47
South Briggs rocks 20
Southampton 100
Southsea 16
Speaker, HMS 93, 95
Spitfire 10, 22, 39, 48, 51, 63, 102
Sri Lanka 73
Strangford Lough 7, 12, 56, 58, *59*, 60
Strangford Lough Yacht Club *8*, 9
Stranraer 13
Stretton 47
Striker, HMS 86
Suez Canal 73, *74–5*
Supermarine 22, 70
Swordfish 37, 102
Sydenham, RNAS 56–7, 64
Sydney 76–7, *78–9*, 80, 93, 94, 99–100
Sydney Daily Telegraph 81
Sydney General Hospital 100

Task Force 57 83
Taranto 102
Taylor, Lt A *85*
Texas, USS 51
Thomas, Sub-Lt R *85*
Thorney Island 53
Thousand Islands 22
Tiger Moth 16–17, *19*, 22, 37, 104
Tojo 99

Tokyo 96, 99
Tokyo Bay 96, *98*, 99
Toronto 24
Townsville 93
Travose Head golf club 39
Trouville 50, 53
Truk 94
Tucker, Lt B *85*
Tugby, Lt D *85*

UK (United Kingdom) 16, 25, 29–30, 70, 89, 100
Ulagh 9
Ulster 58, 64, 104
Ulster TT 7, 9, 39
Undine, HMS 95
Union Club, Belfast 13
USA 37
USAAF 95
US Third Fleet *98*
US Navy (USN) 63

Vercoe, Sub-Lt (A) J *85*, 95
Victorious, HMS 86, 93
Virginia 37
VJ Day 96
Vulture, HMS 39, 42

Wales 31
Wallace, Bill 14, 104
Walrus 40, 94–5
War of 1812 29
Warmwell 36

Warspite, HMS 37
Warwick Farm Racecourse 100
Watertown (New York) 24
Wave King 86
Wave Monarch 86
Weasel 89
Welsh Regiment 11
Whale Island 14, 37
Whimbrel 86
Whiterock 7, *8*, 9, 11–13, 56, *62*
Whylla 89
Wick 44
Wildcat 70
Wilmot, Chief Petty Officer 14
Winchester 36
Woodfield, Sub-Lt W *85*
World War One 36, 64
World War Two 4
Worthy Down, RNAS 36–7, 39, 42

Yalta conference 73
Yeovilton, RNAS 31, *32*, 33, 36